The New York Times

IN THE HEADLINES

Conspiracy Theories

REAL, IMAGINED AND MANUFACTURED

EDUCATIONAL PUBLISHING
BOOKS

THE NEW YORK TIMES EDITORIAL STAFF

**Published in 2020 by New York Times Educational Publishing
in association with The Rosen Publishing Group, Inc.
29 East 21st Street, New York, NY 10010**

First Edition

The New York Times
Alex Ward: Editorial Director, Book Development
Phyllis Collazo: Photo Rights/Permissions Editor
Heidi Giovine: Administrative Manager

Rosen Publishing
Megan Kellerman: Managing Editor
Julia Bosson: Editor
Greg Tucker: Creative Director
Brian Garvey: Art Director

Cataloging-in-Publication Data
Names: New York Times Company.
Title: Conspiracy theories: real, imagined and manufactured / edited by the New York Times editorial staff.
Description: New York : New York Times Educational Publishing, 2020. | Series: In the headlines | Includes glossary and index.
Identifiers: ISBN 9781642822120 (library bound) | ISBN 9781642822113 (pbk.) | ISBN 9781642822137 (ebook)
Subjects: LCSH: Conspiracy theories—Juvenile literature.
Classification: LCC HV6275.C663 2020 | DDC 001.9—dc23

Manufactured in the United States of America

On the cover: President John F. Kennedy and First Lady Jackie Kennedy smile at the crowds lining their motorcade route in Dallas, Tex., on Nov. 22, 1963. Minutes later, the President was assassinated as his car passed through Dealey Plaza; Bettmann/Getty Images.

Contents

CHAPTER 3

Conspiracies on the Right

CHAPTER 4

Donald Trump and the Mainstream Conspiracy Theory

CHAPTER 5

Alex Jones, False Flags and Crisis Actors

Introduction

IN DECEMBER 2016, a man armed with a rifle broke into a Washington, D.C., pizzeria and announced that he was there to investigate rumors of a child sex ring with ties to Hillary Clinton. The story, known as Pizzagate, was a conspiracy theory circulated by fringe websites on the right that originated in a close reading of the campaign emails released by WikiLeaks earlier in the year. Although the rumor had been quickly debunked by experts, the firing of shots inside the pizza shop turned national attention to the story and the community that had promoted it. Conspiracy theories, which have been present in American society since the founding of the republic, have become a part of contemporary political life.

In contemporary American society, conspiracy theories frequently surround the lives of the country's most powerful political figures and rise in the wake of national tragedies. Theorists comb through police reports, F.B.I. records and home-video footage looking for incongruities, seeking evidence that could suggest ulterior narratives. The logic of these conspiracies is sometimes compelling, sometimes ludicrous, but it always finds an audience. The Internet has provided a platform to conspiracy enthusiasts of all stripes, offering spaces for theorists to connect and tools to dissect potential clues. However, along with the growth of online conspiracy communities, some theories have made their way out from the recesses of message boards and into the mainstream.

Perhaps no event during the 20th century resulted in more conspiracy theories than the assassination of President John F. Kennedy. In the more than 50 years since he was shot in a motorcade in Dallas, dozens of rumors have circulated, suggesting a wide variety

JOE TABACCA FOR THE NEW YORK TIMES

Marchers were among the 500 conspiracy theorists at a two-day Chicago convention in early June 2006 calling for what they considered "9/11 truth."

of complicated evidence and potential intrigue. From ballistics analysis to a closely dissected video, believers have examined and re-examined the evidence, seeing possibilities of Mafia connections, a Cuban plot or even an inside job. When the F.B.I. declassified many of the files relating to their investigation in 2017, curiosity was renewed, although proof of conspiracy was scant.

The events of Sept. 11, 2001, inspired similar debates. Some far left groups saw the attack on the World Trade Center as a possible impetus for war, while other theorists analyzed the pattern of explosions and the structure of the buildings, suggesting that the buildings could not have fallen on their own with outside explosives. In a movement that became known as the "truther" movement, 9/11 conspiracy theorists pointed to signs of controlled demolitions, occasionally making headlines through protests and incendiary documentaries.

In recent years, however, conspiracies have begun to more broadly impact mainstream political discourse. The individual most responsible for this might be Alex Jones of Infowars, a media company known for spreading a variety of far-right conspiracy theories. In recent years, Jones has gained notoriety for calling into question the validity of mass shootings, suggesting survivors and family members were paid actors in a leftist plot for gun control. In 2018, his targeting of Sandy Hook family members earned him his first prohibition from YouTube, Facebook and Twitter, a watershed moment in the Internet's censuring of conspiracies.

One of Jones's listeners is President Donald J. Trump, who, during his time in office, has promoted stories that have been firmly debunked by experts. Before his election, Trump vocally endorsed a theory that President Obama was born in Kenya, which would have invalidated his candidacy for presidency. Known as "birtherism," the movement repeatedly called for Obama to present his birth certificate, and continued well after Obama presented it.

The challenge that conspiracy theories pose to media companies such as The New York Times is immense. News organizations must decide how to cover these conspiracies, analyzing them without giving them credence or expanding their platform. In the articles collected here, journalists cover the spread of conspiracy theories as well as their consequences, navigating the line between truth, theory, belief and falsehood.

CHAPTER 1

Who Shot J.F.K.?

Any discussion of American conspiracy theories must begin with the J.F.K. assassination. On Nov. 22, 1963, President John F. Kennedy was shot as he rode in a motorcade in Dallas. Although experts have concluded that the gunman, Lee Harvey Oswald, acted alone, there were enough peculiarities to inspire a breadth of conspiracy theories, from rumors of a second gunman to hints of Mafia connections. In 2017, President Trump ordered the declassification of a trove of F.B.I. documents regarding the assassination, opening the door to renewed speculation.

28 Years After Kennedy's Assassination, Conspiracy Theories Refuse to Die

BY CLIFFORD KRAUSS | JAN. 5, 1992

NEARLY THREE DECADES after the assassination of President John F. Kennedy, the film director Oliver Stone has revitalized an American obsession with conspiracies.

Mr. Stone's movie "J.F.K." liberally mixes fiction with fact, and some have dismissed it as an outrageous distortion of history. But the monstrous web of political, government and corporate interests that the film portrays as being behind the killing does reflect widely held suspicions that more than a single gunman was responsible for the slaying.

Public opinion polls taken over the last several years have shown that fewer than one-third of the American people accept the findings of the Warren Commission that Lee Harvey Oswald acted alone. Unanswered questions about the investigations and the disposition of certain evidence, like autopsy notes that were burned, have only fed the doubts.

A LAWMAKER'S DOUBT

"Will we ever know all the facts and circumstances?" asked Representative Louis Stokes, Democrat of Ohio, the chairman of the former House Select Committee on Assassinations, which conducted its investigation into the slaying in the late 1970's. "No. We don't know all the facts and circumstances about the Lincoln assassination."

Conspiracy theories began to circulate almost immediately after President Kennedy was shot, when broadcast commentators reporting the shooting speculated that Dallas right-wingers might have plotted to kill him on that sunny Friday afternoon in November 1963.

Since then, the Mafia, Cuba, the Soviet Union, the Central Intelligence Agency and the Federal Bureau of Investigation have been linked to the crime, both in purportedly serious investigations as well as in various expressions of pop culture over the years.

"MacBird!", a 1960's off-Broadway play, held Lyndon B. Johnson responsible. A recent documentary broadcast by the A&E cable television network asserted that Oswald was innocent and that three mob contract killers from France shot the President.

A HASTY INVESTIGATION

Arthur Schlesinger Jr., a historian and former adviser to Kennedy, noted that "Americans have been susceptible to conspiracy theories" since at least the 1830's when many Americans thought Masonic plotters were trying to take over the country. He said this susceptibility to paranoia was fortified in the Kennedy case by the fact that the Warren Commission investigation was hasty and incomplete.

"Whether a more adequate investigation would have produced a different conclusion," Mr. Schlesinger said, "is a matter of question."

A kaleidescope of possible motives for the assassination ranges from right-wing disgust at Kennedy's civil rights record to left-wing anger at his Administration's attempts to kill President Fidel Castro of Cuba. Complicating the task of determining a motive are the varying interpretations ascribed to the actions of both Kennedy and Oswald.

Much of the available evidence clouds the issue. James J. Humes, the surgeon who performed the autopsy on Kennedy, burned his notes from the procedure, saying later that he did not think they were important. In addition, the President's brain was lost after it was examined by doctors. Some witnesses to the assassination told investigators they heard three shots; others said they heard four, one of which was fired from a grassy knoll. Then there is the question of why Jack Ruby, a strip-tease club owner with mob connections, killed Oswald if not to protect a conspiracy.

Conspiracy buffs say a home movie filmed by Abraham Zapruder, a dress manufacturer at Dealey Plaza the day of the assassination, dispels the Warren Commission contention that one gunman could have hit Kennedy and Gov. John B. Connally of Texas with the same bullet. But scientific tests commissioned by Congress have shown that fragments found in the Governor's wrist match a bullet that passed through Kennedy.

OFFICIAL VERSIONS

Panel Is Named With Goal in Mind

Johnson appointed a commission headed by Chief Justice Earl Warren to investigate the assassination and calm the public. After interviewing more than 500 witnesses and reviewing hundreds of documents, it concluded that Oswald fired all three shots at Kennedy from the sixth floor of the Texas School Book Depository Building overlooking Dealey Plaza. Citing among other things his palmprint found on the rifle used in the shooting, the commission concluded that Oswald acted alone.

The Warren Commission report has been much maligned over the years as a rush job at best and a piece of a grand Government conspiracy at worst. Critics have noted that the C.I.A. withheld much relevant information from the commission to avert revelations of its efforts, using Mafia connections, to kill Mr. Castro and destabilize his Government.

Senator Arlen Specter, Republican of Pennsylvania, who was an assistant counsel to the commission, said in a recent interview: "I think the commission did a good job. Had there been a conspiracy, I think it would have come to light long ago. You can't keep secrets in America."

A 1979 report by a House Select Committee on Assassinations agreed with the commission that there was no conspiracy involving the Soviet Union, Cuba or a Federal agency, but it suggested that organized crime might have been involved. It also raised doubts about the one-gunman theory. After examining audio tapes taken from a police motorcycle in Dealey Plaza, in combination with testimony from witnesses, it concluded there was a second gunman, who fired a fourth shot from the grassy knoll. That shot missed.

But three years later a panel of the National Academy of Sciences suggested that the audio tape did not support the theory of a second gunman. It reported that the noises earlier said to be gunshots had actually been made a minute after Kennedy was shot. It also suggested that the noises might have been nothing more than radio static.

Representative Stokes, however, said he stood by his panel's findings.

MAFIA CONSPIRACY

Mob Had Reasons And the Ways

Conspiracy theorists have long noted that the Mafia had a motive to destroy the Kennedy Administration. Several Mafia leaders were openly upset with the President's failure to overthrow Mr. Castro, who had closed their lucrative casinos in Havana. In addition, Attorney General Robert F. Kennedy had begun an aggressive campaign against James R. Hoffa, the president of the International Brotherhood of Teamsters who was closely associated with the criminal underworld.

The House assassinations committee suggested that the most likely mob leaders to have participated in the plot were Carlos Marcello of New Orleans, a close associate of Mr. Hoffa who was briefly deported to Central America by the Kennedy Administration, and Santo Trafficante of Havana, who was once jailed by Mr. Castro.

Both Oswald and Ruby had Mafia ties. In his book "The Crisis Years" (HarperCollins, 1991), Michael R. Beschloss noted that in the months before the assassination Oswald stayed at the New Orleans home of his uncle, Charles Murret, a bookmaker with mob connections. When Oswald was arrested during a street fight arising out of a pro-Castro demonstration in August 1963, he was probably bailed out of prison by a Marcello associate, Mr. Beschloss wrote.

According to a 1950's Senate investigation of the underworld, Ruby was a liaison between various groups in the Chicago mob. He evidentally ran guns for the Mafia to anti-Castro guerrillas. As the conspiracy theory goes, Ruby was sent by the mob to kill Oswald before he could talk. In a polygraph test taken in prison, however, Ruby denied that he was part of a conspiracy and that he knew Oswald.

"There is one key fact at the center of this," said Jonathan Kwitny, an investigative reporter who said he based his conclusions on documents gathered by the House committee and independent inquiries in which he took part. "Once you learn that Jack Ruby and Lee Oswald were both working for the Marcello organization in the months before the assassination and you know that Marcello had the strongest motive for killing Kennedy, it may not be proof, but you have to start there."

Senator Specter said he did not think it was plausible that the mob hired either Oswald or Ruby because they were "unstable and unreliable."

COMMUNIST CONSPIRACY

Assassin's Ties To Soviet World

Oswald's shady connections extended as far as Moscow, although few analysts have taken seriously the possibility that the Soviet

Union ordered Kennedy killed. After serving in the Marine Corps, Oswald defected to the Soviet Union in 1959 for two years. There he married a Russian woman named Marina whose uncle was reportedly an officer in the secret police. Disillusioned with the drabness of Soviet life, he applied for readmission to the United States with his wife.

Back in the United States, Oswald expressed interest in the activities of the Communist Party and a pro-Castro organization. He passed out pro-Castro literature in the streets of New Orleans and traveled to Mexico in an unsuccessful effort to gain entrance to Cuba.

At a news conference at the Brazilian Embassy in Havana only two months before Kennedy was killed, Mr. Castro said, "United States leaders should think that if they are aiding terrorist plans to eliminate Cuban leaders, they themselves will not be safe."

In her Castro biography, "Guerrilla Prince" (Little, Brown, 1991), the columnist Georgie Anne Geyer wrote, "There are simply too many 'accidents' not to assume that there could have been some Castro involvement. Oswald was seen at private parties conversing with Mexican Communists and with Cuban diplomats."

In a variation on Ms. Geyer's contention, Daniel Schorr, the broadcast journalist, noted in his 1977 book "Clearing the Air" (Houghton Mifflin) that Oswald could have read a news service dispatch in a New Orleans newspaper reporting Mr. Castro's vague threat and taken it upon himself to kill Kennedy to help Cuba.

Johnson said on various occasions that he thought Mr. Castro was behind the assassination, a charge the Cuban leader has repeatedly denied.

Mr. Stokes, who as chairman of the assassinations panel traveled to Cuba in 1978 to question Mr. Castro, returned saying he believed the Cuban leader's disclaimers. "Castro summed it up best himself," Mr. Stokes said, "He said, 'I would have to be crazy. They would blow my little country off the map.' "

GOVERNMENT CONSPIRACY

Intriguing Links In a Bizarre Theory

Of all the conspiracy theories, the most bizarre allege a sweeping plot that included the F.B.I., the C.I.A., the Pentagon or the Secret Service, or all of the above. One variation, promoted by Mark North in his book "Act of Treason" (Carroll & Graf, 1991), argues that J. Edgar Hoover, Director of the F.B.I., learned of the plot in advance but did nothing to protect the President.

In "J.F.K." Mr. Stone has popularized what his critics argue is the most paranoid vision of America, one in which a fascistic elite murdered the President. The film dramatizes the investigations of Jim Garrison, a former New Orleans District Attorney who asserted that the Warren Commission report was a tissue of lies, a coverup for an intelligence agency cell consisting largely of right-wing Cubans who carried out the assassination. Their motive was both to propel the Vietnam War and to establish a more vigorous policy to overthrow Mr. Castro.

Mr. Garrison's 1967 prosecution against Clay Shaw, a New Orleans businessman who he said had plotted with Oswald and others to kill Kennedy, ended when a jury found Mr. Shaw not guilty.

But some conspiracy theorists still argue that he was on to something. They point out that Mr. Shaw is now known to have been a C.I.A. contact although he had denied having dealings with the agency. They note that the man Mr. Garrison accused of being a co-conspirator, David Ferrie, a former airline pilot who dropped dead during the investigation, had been seen consulting with Carlos Marcello shortly before the Kennedy assassination. And, finally, they argue that it is more than coincidence that a third man accused of being a co-conspirator, Guy W. Banister, a former F.B.I. agent and anti-Castro worker, had an office in a building whose address was on pro-Castro literature passed out by Oswald.

DISPARAGED BY ANALYSTS

Such theories are disparaged by an assortment of analysts. Mr. Kwitny said the Garrison and Stone school "convert Kennedy into a flower child" when he was really a cold warrior. Mr. Kwitny suggested that the intelligence agency and other Federal agencies covered up evidence to avert disclosure of their contacts with the Mafia to kill Mr. Castro, as well as information linking Oswald to American intelligence. "But that doesn't mean they were involved in the crime," he said.

Mr. Kwitny said Oswald, who learned Russian as a marine, was probably inserted in the Soviet Union as a spy, a fact the Government would not have wanted the public and the Soviets to know.

For "J.F.K." to be true, Robert Kennedy, as Attorney General, "would have had to have been a part of or indifferent to the conspiracy," Senator Specter said, adding, "That's ridiculous."

Conspiracy theories will swirl until the C.I.A., the F.B.I. and Congress release all files related to the assassination. Saying that much of the information in the reports it gathered is full of rumors that will only muddy the matter further, the House plans to disclose all its documents only in 2029.

Even after all the documents are made public, many analysts said, there will still be people who believe there has been a Government coverup.

"There isn't a single witness left to bring in," said G. Robert Blakey, the chief counsel to the House investigation. "The people out there are all people with theories."

Mystery From the Grave Beside Oswald's, Solved

BY DAN BARRY | AUG. 9, 2013

FORT WORTH — In a corner of the Shannon Rose Hill Cemetery, close to a chain-link fence that separates the living and the dead, a patch of ground has been worn free of grass by all who come to stare at one particular gravestone. With just a surname, the marker says it all: OSWALD.

But in the half-century since a slight, sallow man named Lee Harvey Oswald killed President John F. Kennedy, so much continues to be said about the assassination that the various conspiracy devices and theories are nearly as familiar as the tragic event itself. The Magic Bullet theory. The Zapruder film. The Umbrella Man. The Mafia. Jack Ruby. Fidel Castro.

And, of course, Nick Beef. Or, more accurately, NICK BEEF.

For the last 15 years, this curious name has vexed the obsessive assassination buffs who make regular pilgrimages to the Oswald plot here in Fort Worth. That is because a pinkish granite marker suddenly appeared beside the assassin's grave sometime in 1997. And all it said was Nick Beef.

In their quest to make sense of a national catastrophe — to find a narrative more acceptable than that of one gunman, acting alone — some theorists have tried to divine meaning in a name that, more than anything else, evokes a private eye who specializes in agricultural intrigue. It added another question to their already exhausting list. Who *was* Nick Beef?

To begin with, Mr. Beef remains happily above the clay.

Affable, with gray-black hair slicked back, save for a stray curl or two, he sips tea at a cozy table at the Jack bistro in Greenwich Village, not far from his Manhattan apartment. With evident pride in possessing one of the more distinctive conversation starters in American

REX C. CURRY FOR THE NEW YORK TIMES

Conspiracy theorists have been intrigued for years by the marker beside Lee Harvey Oswald's. They might be disappointed.

discourse, he confirms that he owns the burial plot beside Lee Harvey Oswald's.

As for his notoriety among the conspiracy cognoscenti, he says, he came by it innocently, even accidentally. But now, with the 50th anniversary of the Kennedy assassination less than four months away, he has decided to reveal himself, sort of, to The New York Times.

This scoop may not definitively link Castro, the mob, and the Central Intelligence Agency to the Kennedy assassination, but, hey, it's something. And to prove that he is who he says he is, Mr. Beef reaches into a small satchel and pulls out a contract from 1975 for Burial Plot 258 in the Fairlawn section of Rose Hill ($175), as well as a receipt from 1996 for the purchase and installation of a granite stone to be engraved NICK BEEF ($987.19).

Mr. Beef, 56, is a writer and "nonperforming performance artist" with a penchant for the morbid, he says, who has never done stand-up comedy — an important point. He says that Nick Beef is a long-held persona; his given name is Patric Abedin. Here is his story.

On Nov. 21, 1963, President Kennedy and his wife, Jacqueline, landed at the former Carswell Air Force Base in Fort Worth as part of a two-day Texas tour. Among the many gathered for the arrival — some holding "Welcome to Texas, Jack and Jackie" signs — was young Patric, the 6-year-old asthmatic son of an Air Force navigator. Having gotten lost in the crowd, the boy was sitting on the shoulders of a military police officer when the first couple passed by just a few feet away.

The future Mr. Beef was Mr. Popular the next morning at Waverly Park Elementary School, as he regaled his first-grade classmates with his presidential story. They soon went outside for recess, while his asthma kept him indoors. He was alone, then, when the principal announced over the loudspeaker that the president had been shot; alone, too, when the principal followed up to say that the president was dead.

As his class returned from recess, he told his teacher what he had heard. At first she suspected that he was vying for more attention. But soon, as everyone of a certain age remembers, classes were abruptly dismissed amid the weeping of teachers.

A young boy's life continued. His father took him to the World's Fair in New York. His older brother broke his jaw during some horseplay. His parents divorced. At the age of 10, he survived a car crash that killed a 9-year-old friend.

The lesson he was learning: "Things change really quickly."

By the late 1960s, he was living with his remarried mother in Arlington, Tex. Every week they would drive to the Carswell base for his free asthma shot, then occasionally stop at the eclectic cemetery called Rose Hill on their way home. "She'd get out and look at Oswald's grave," he recalls, "and tell me, 'Never forget that you got to see Kennedy the night before he died.' "

The years passed. When he was 18, he read a newspaper article's passing mention that the grave beside Oswald's had never been purchased. He went to Rose Hill, where a caretaker in a glorified garden shed thumbed through some cards and said, "Yep, that's available."

The young man put $17.50 down, and promised to make 16 monthly payments of $10.

Mr. Beef has often asked himself why. "It meant something to me in life," is the only answer he can come up with. "It was a place I could go and feel comfortable."

Around the same time, he and a friend were trying to make each other laugh while driving to Dallas from Lubbock. Stopping at a bar and grill, his friend decided to become Hash Brown; he declared himself Nick Beef. A joke.

As for his unmarked burial plot back in Rose Hill, he says: "I just sat on it. Not literally."

Life followed its unpredictable course. He worked for a local television station, moved to New York, got involved with a sketch-comedy troupe called the Other Leading Brand. He did some freelance humor writing, sometimes using the byline of Nick Beef. He married, had two children, and amicably divorced. Somewhere in there, Oswald's body was exhumed to address speculation that the buried remains were actually those of a Russian agent; they were not.

In late 1996, Mr. Beef's mother died, and he returned to Texas to follow the detailed instructions she had left for her own funeral. During his stay, he visited his real estate in Rose Hill and decided, on the spot, to buy a gravestone the exact dimensions as Oswald's. When the cemetery official asked what he wanted on it, he thought about protecting his two children.

"Well, here we go," he recalls thinking.

Upon hearing the name, the official put down his pen. But he picked it up again when the customer pulled out a credit card in the name of Nick Beef.

With the gravestone planted, rumors and speculation took root. It was said that since the cemetery refuses to provide directions to Oswald's grave — at the family's request, a spokeswoman for the cemetery said — two reporters had bought the plot so that the curious could ask instead for Nick Beef. It was also said that Nick Beef was a New York stand-up comic who used references to the grave in his act. Assassination buffs swapped theories on the Internet.

Meanwhile, Mr. Beef just carried on, not answering e-mails or telephone calls or the doorbell's persistent buzz. He began creating photographic haikus by using snapshots of tombstones that he had taken; he calls his work "DieKus." For example:

Bishop. Block. Castle.
Knight. Leap. Castle. Spear. Bishop.
Queen. Downs. King. Chek. Mate.

Yes, he admits again, he has a penchant for the morbid. But this does not mean that he bought the plot next to Oswald's as a joke, or a piece of installation art, or anything of the kind. It's personal. It's about change. The fragility of life. Something.

And no, Nick Beef will not be buried inches from the man who killed Kennedy.

"I'd prefer to be cremated," he says.

No Stranger to Conspiracy

OPINION | BY DAN BARRY | AUG. 17, 2013

AS A VETERAN newspaper reporter, I've heard some things. I once sat in a Friendly's restaurant in Connecticut with an earnest nun who, between sips of her Fribble, confided that an evil man who looked like Pope Paul VI — but who was not Pope Paul VI — had seized control of the Vatican in the 1960s. A papal double, she explained. And she had photographs to prove it.

I knocked back a double Fribble and asked for the check.

Journalists will entertain conspiracy theories because conspiracies, in fact, do take place, and at our best we seek out the stories behind the stories. But we also pay a price if we don't buy into every one. If you write that Neil Armstrong walked on the moon in the summer of 1969, some reader somewhere is guaranteed to call you a government dupe. Hey, Jimmy Olsen! Everyone knows that Armstrong took one giant leap on a secured movie lot. Sap.

Though I am not unfamiliar with being called a patsy, I still respect and admire those who challenge the conventional wisdom; this is how I was raised, as you will see. Even so, I was still cold-cocked by the response to a recent This Land column of mine that touched on the assassination of President John F. Kennedy in 1963.

Holy Zapruder.

The column focused on Patric Abedin, who owns a Fort Worth burial plot right beside Lee Harvey Oswald's. The granite marker he placed above the empty grave says NICK BEEF, a curious name that has prompted years of Internet speculation. Let's just say that Mr. Abedin, or Mr. Beef, has his reasons, going back to when he was a boy and saw President Kennedy at an Air Force base the night before the assassination.

In the column, I referred in passing to Oswald as the man who killed Kennedy. I did not use the phrase "alleged assassin." I did not attribute the reference to the Warren Commission. I simply wrote that Oswald assassinated Kennedy, thinking that nearly 50 years have passed — a half-century! — and no one else has been convincingly tied to the murder.

So began my refresher course. While some readers wrote to say nice job and have a nice day, others got right to the point: I was a government patsy, employed by a newspaper that has worked in concert with various insidious powers to suppress what really happened in Dallas. One reader charged me with a "virtually treasonous act."

The rough consensus among these unhappy readers was that at least two gunmen were involved, and that the Warren Commission was inept at best, corrupt at worst. In addition, I was a thought-free tool — a sap, really — who, among other failures, had made no reference to the House Select Committee on Assassinations report of 1979, which concluded that while Oswald fired the fatal shot, there also existed the probability of a conspiracy among unknown participants.

It might spawn another conspiracy belief for my critics to learn that I am of proud conspiracy-theorist stock. While other fathers pursued hobbies like golf, mine spent his free time trying to expose a government cover-up of the existence of U.F.O.'s. His preferred family outing was to pull over the station wagon and search the night skies for extraterrestrial activity.

That's how we Barrys rolled.

My father was also obsessed with the murder of Kennedy, one of his few heroes. Our family bible was not the Bible but Mark Lane's "Rush to Judgment," a sort of conspiracy primer on the assassination. Other children discussed the films of Walt Disney; my siblings and I discussed the film of Abraham Zapruder.

As time moved on, though, my questions about the Kennedy assassination gave in to a general acceptance that Oswald had acted alone. Probably.

But a half-century after the tragedy, I remain in the minority. According to an Associated Press-GfK poll conducted earlier this year,

59 percent of Americans believe in an assassination conspiracy. Presumably, that includes my three siblings.

At least I am in fast company. Among the nonbelievers is the prominent presidential historian Robert Dallek, whose most recent book, "Camelot's Court: Inside the Kennedy White House," is one of many Kennedy books coming out in time for the assassination's 50th anniversary in November.

"If there was some grand conspiracy, it would have been outed by now," he said.

Mr. Dallek is more intrigued by the apparent need to believe in a conspiracy. "They can't accept that someone as inconsequential as Oswald could have killed someone as consequential as Kennedy," he said. "To believe that only Oswald killed Kennedy — that there wasn't some larger plot — shows people how random the world is, how uncertain. And I think it pains them; they don't want to accept that fact."

Jesse Walker, the books editor at Reason magazine and the author of "The United States of Paranoia," also to be released in the coming days, said that conspiracy theories have a long and potent history in this country and are hardly embraced by only the fringe.

"Conspiracy theories emerge at this place where our natural tendency to find patterns and tell stories meets our natural tendency to have suspicions and fears," he said.

Now and then I think of that nun at Friendly's all those years ago. More often, I think of my father, who taught me about Watergate and other true conspiracies, dying without seeing a U.F.O. or trusting the official story of how his hero had died.

The murder of a president has not been easy for any of us who remember it.

"I love my country and find it hard to shrug and 'move on,' " one of the more thoughtful conspiracy theorists wrote to me. "Good luck to us all."

DAN BARRY is a national correspondent who writes the This Land column for The New York Times.

The J.F.K. Files: Decades of Doubts and Conspiracy Theories

BY LORI MOORE | OCT. 25, 2017

THE GRANDDADDY OF all conspiracy theories has re-emerged in the American psyche with the planned release of the National Archives's final trove of records about the assassination of President John F. Kennedy.

Kennedy's death on Nov. 22, 1963, and the numerous investigations that followed were simultaneously some of the most secretive and public events in modern history.

The last of the sealed government papers relating to the assassination are expected to be made public by Thursday, after President Trump announced last week that he would not block their release.

Government agencies, Hollywood big shots and amateur sleuths have floated theories of what happened to Kennedy: a plot by Cold War adversaries like Cuba and the Soviet Union; an elaborate mafia-backed hit; a covert federal government coup. And it's been going on for over 50 years.

'A WOUND IN THE BRAIN'

Kennedy's was one of the most public murders in history, a victim shot in front of hundreds of spectators, with a coterie of news reporters in tow. Page One of The Times blared the news of the assassination, reporting that "he died of a wound in the brain caused by a rifle bullet that was fired at him as he was riding through downtown Dallas in a motorcade."

The report chronicled the swift chaos of the day, from Kennedy's pre-breakfast speech to Lyndon B. Johnson's swearing-in as president on Air Force One a few hours later.

Mr. Johnson, who was uninjured in the shooting, took his oath in the Presidential jet plane as it stood on the runway at Love Field. The body of Mr.

Kennedy was aboard. Immediately after the oath-taking, the plane took off for Washington.

Standing beside the new President as Mr. Johnson took the oath of office was Mrs. John F. Kennedy. Her stockings were spattered with her husband's blood.

LEE HARVEY OSWALD

"Lee H. Oswald, who once defected to the Soviet Union and who has been active in the Fair Play for Cuba Committee, was arrested by the Dallas police," The Times reported on the same front page. "Tonight he was accused of the killing."

Immediately after the shooting, a witness told reporters that as "shots rang out he saw a rifle extended and then withdrawn from a window on the "fifth or sixth floor" of the Texas School Book Depository.

Oswald, a former Marine, had become "a changed man with a new and bewildering personality when he returned to the United States in 1962," according to his wife, Marina, whom he married while living in Russia.

He was famously shot dead by Jack Ruby while in police custody on Nov. 24, two days after the assassination.

THE WARREN COMMISSION: DISCREDITING 'MYTHS'

A week after Kennedy's death, Johnson convened a government body to investigate it, led by Chief Justice Earl Warren.

The nearly yearlong investigation included the private testimony of Jacqueline Kennedy. Many of the findings, like the infamous "magic-bullet theory," have been contested.

Ultimately, the commission ruled that Oswald had acted alone, rejecting any idea that Russia or Cuba officially backed him, but demanded reforms from the F.B.I. and the Secret Service.

The commission, saying that the " 'publicizing of unchecked information' had led to 'myths' and 'distorted' interpretations," also tried to discredit the multiplying conspiracy theories behind the assassination. It didn't work.

INVESTIGATED AGAIN. AND AGAIN.

At least two more official federal government panels convened in the 1960s and '70s to relitigate the shooting. In 1969, Attorney General Ramsey Clark appointed four medical experts to re-examine scientific evidence, in part as a response to an investigation by the New Orleans district attorney, Jim Garrison. Clark's panel backed the Warren Commission's assertion that only two bullets had killed the president.

In 1979, the House Select Committee on Assassinations, dogged by internal strife during its two and a half years of existence, released a report saying that untold conspirators had probably participated in the killing, citing newly uncovered evidence and scientific advances.

> *According to the committee, Oswald fired three shots from the sixth floor window of the Texas School Book Depository Building and an unidentified person fired one shot from the grassy knoll in front of the President's limousine.*

The committee cited witnesses in its findings of a second gunman, including:

> *... a police officer who said he heard a shot from the knoll and ran immediately toward it. There he encountered a man who said he was with the Secret Service and displayed a badge, which the policemen did not inspect very closely.*
>
> *A check of the placement of Secret Service agents, however, disclosed that none had been in the area of the knoll.*

Over the years, the Warren Commission findings remained in doubt in some circles. In 1988, David W. Belin, a lawyer who had advised the commission, wrote:

> *Yet 25 years after the event, a majority of the American public does not believe the truth. Rather, polls have shown that most Americans believe President Kennedy was assassinated as an outgrowth of a conspiracy.*

In 1991, the conspiracy reignited in the form of a major Hollywood movie.

'J.F.K.' AND REWRITING HISTORY

In 1969, a jury took only 50 minutes to acquit a man named Clay Shaw of conspiring to assassinate Kennedy.

The Oliver Stone movie "J.F.K." in 1991 reimagined both that 34-day trial, called a "circus" by many, and the extensive investigation by Garrison, the New Orleans district attorney.

As The Times wrote in Garrison's 1992 obituary:

> *Announcing that he had "solved the assassination," Mr. Garrison accused anti-Communist and anti-Castro extremists in the Central Intelligence Agency of plotting the President's death to thwart an easing of tension with the Soviet Union and Cuba, and to prevent a retreat from Vietnam.*

Garrison, whom The Times described in a lengthy 1967 profile as a headline-seeking crusader with political aspirations long before the Shaw trial, was an adviser for the film, which renewed calls for answers but was criticized by many as a rewriting of history.

Mr. Stone addressed these accusations in a Times Op-Ed:

> *My critics are outraged that I pose the view that Kennedy's desire to wind down the cold war and the Vietnam War is a possible motive for the murder. When a leader of any country is assassinated, the media normally ask: "What political forces were opposed to this leader and would benefit from his assassination?"*

The film is partly credited with the passage, the year after it was released, of the President John F. Kennedy Assassination Records Collection Act. The law mandated the release of all the government archives on the assassination within 25 years, by Oct. 26, 2017.

CASE CLOSED? IT'S MORE COMPLICATED THAN THAT

Thousands of records have been declassified since, many shedding more light on American foreign policy than on the assassination. Some files detailed the president's plans to exit the conflict in Vietnam; others showed how Fidel Castro feared the United States would retaliate against Cuba after the assassination. A large trove uncovered the ideas — ranging from the rote to the James Bond-like — that the Pentagon had floated for dealing with Cuba.

Public interest in the most recent release by the National Archives, in July 2017, nearly crashed its servers, Politico reported.

The release of the final papers may only fuel more conspiracy theories, as did the first set of files, made public in 1993:

> *For those who believe that the assassination was the sole work of Oswald, an ex-marine who had failed in nearly every endeavor, including an attempt to defect to Moscow, the newly released documents offer the final proof. And for those who believe that Oswald did not act alone, the documents also offer substantiation.*
>
> *"This will feed another generation of assassination buffs, the children of assassination buffs," said Edward Jay Epstein, who wrote three books and an anthology on the assassination.*

J.F.K. Files, Though Incomplete, Are a Treasure Trove for Answer Seekers

BY PETER BAKER AND SCOTT SHANE | OCT. 26, 2017

WASHINGTON — President Trump ordered the long-awaited release on Thursday of more than 2,800 documents related to the assassination of President John F. Kennedy, but bowed to pressure from the C.I.A. and F.B.I. by withholding thousands of additional papers pending six more months of review.

While incomplete, the documents were a treasure trove for investigators, historians and conspiracy theorists who have spent half a century searching for clues to what really happened in Dallas on that fateful day in 1963. They included tantalizing talk of mobsters and Cubans and spies, Kremlin suspicions that Lyndon B. Johnson was behind the killing, and fear among the authorities that the public would not accept the official version of events.

Paging through the documents online on Thursday night was a little like exploring a box of random papers found in an attic. There were fuzzy images of C.I.A. surveillance photos from the early 1960s; a log from December 1963 of visitors, including a C.I.A. officer, to Johnson's ranch in Texas; and reports that Lee Harvey Oswald obtained ammunition from a right-wing militia group.

Some of the documents convey some of the drama and chaos of the days immediately after the murder of the president. Among them is a memo apparently dictated by J. Edgar Hoover, the F.B.I. director, on Nov. 24, 1963, shortly after Jack Ruby shot and killed Oswald as he was being moved from Police Headquarters to a local jail.

"There is nothing further on the Oswald case except that he is dead," the memo begins laconically, before reciting the day's events.

Mr. Trump, who has indulged in his own wild speculation about the sensational killing, had expressed eagerness to finally open the last of the government files, only to run into a last-minute campaign by intelligence agencies to redact certain documents. Grudgingly, he gave the agencies until April 26 to go through the remaining papers again and make their case.

"I am ordering today that the veil finally be lifted," Mr. Trump said in a memo to the agencies. Given their objections, he said, "I have no choice — today — but to accept those redactions rather than allow potentially irreversible harm to our nation's security." But he ordered the agencies to "be extremely circumspect," noting that the rationale for secrecy has only "grown weaker with the passage of time."

For conspiracy theorists, the Kennedy assassination has been the holy grail, one that has produced an endless string of books, reports, lectures, articles, websites, documentaries and big-screen Hollywood movies. It was the first murder of an American president in the television age, touching off a wave of global grief for a charismatic young leader while also spawning a cottage industry of skeptical questioning of the official version of events.

Every government authority that has examined the investigation of his death, from the Warren Commission to congressional investigators, concluded that Kennedy was killed by Oswald, who fired three shots with a mail-order rifle from the sixth floor of the Texas School Book Depository when the presidential motorcade passed by on Nov. 22, 1963. But that has never satisfied the doubters, and polls have consistently shown that most Americans still believe that someone other than Oswald must have been involved.

While the Warren Commission concluded that Oswald acted alone, the House Select Committee on Assassinations said in a 1979 report that Kennedy "was probably assassinated as a result of a conspiracy" but did not identify who those conspirators might have been. It ruled out the Soviet and Cuban governments, organized Cubans opposing Fidel Castro, the Mafia, the F.B.I., the C.I.A. and the Secret Service, although the committee said it could not preclude that individuals affiliated with some of those groups might have been involved.

Among the doubters have been Mr. Trump, who last year alleged that the father of one of his Republican presidential primary rivals, Senator Ted Cruz of Texas, was somehow involved in the assassination. The president's longtime friend and adviser Roger J. Stone Jr. wrote a book accusing Johnson of being responsible for the shooting that elevated him to the presidency.

As it happened, Mr. Trump's deferral to the C.I.A. and F.B.I. invariably will lead to suspicions that the government is still protecting sensational secrets about the case. Administration officials said there was no cover-up, just an effort to avoid compromising national security, law enforcement or intelligence gathering methods.

The C.I.A., which for years has borne the brunt of suspicions from amateur assassination theorists, went out of its way on Thursday to try to dispel concerns that it was hiding important evidence.

The agency issued a statement noting that the vast majority of assassination-related records have been released, and that redactions were intended "to protect information in the collection whose disclosure would harm national security — including the names of C.I.A. assets and current and former C.I.A. officers, as well as specific intelligence methods and partnerships that remain viable to protecting the nation today."

The release of the documents owes as much to the moviemaker Oliver Stone as anyone else. After his 1991 conspiracy theory movie "J.F.K." stoked renewed interest, Congress passed the President John F. Kennedy Assassination Records Collection Act, which was signed into law by President George Bush on Oct. 26, 1992. The act mandated that all assassination records be released no later than 25 years from that date, which was Thursday, unless the president authorized further withholding for national security reasons.

In the years since the law was passed, the National Archives and Records Administration has released 88 percent of those documents in full and an additional 11 percent with portions redacted. Until Thursday, just 1 percent had been withheld in full.

Of the 2,891 documents released Thursday, only 53 had never been disclosed by the archives; the rest had been made public with redactions.

The papers range widely, and while many are not directly related to the assassination, others add context. One recounted the reaction of the Soviet Union to the killing, reporting that some in Moscow assumed it was a "coup" by the "ultraright" that would be blamed on the Soviet Union. An unnamed informant told American spies that the K.G.B. had proof that "President Johnson was responsible for the assassination."

An F.B.I. cable from April 1964 reconstructed Oswald's bus trip to Mexico weeks before the assassination, including the names of the people sitting around him and even what he was wearing: "a short-sleeved light colored sport shirt and no coat."

In Hoover's memo two days after the assassination, he expressed anxiety that Oswald's killing would generate doubts among Americans. "The thing I am concerned about," he wrote, "is having something issued so that we can convince the public that Oswald is the real assassin." The F.B.I. director also fretted that discoveries that Oswald contacted the Cuban Embassy in Mexico City and sent a letter to the Soviet Embassy in Washington could "complicate our foreign relations."

He called the Oswald killing "inexcusable" in light of "our warnings to the Dallas Police Department" and hinted at Ruby's mob connections, which would soon spawn an industry of research and speculation. "We have no information on Ruby that is firm, although there are some rumors of underworld activity in Chicago," Hoover wrote.

The documents will not end the debate or speculation — and a few may add to the questions. In a 1975 deposition, for example, Richard Helms, the former C.I.A. director, was asked: "Is there any information involved with the assassination of President Kennedy which in any way shows that Lee Harvey Oswald was in some way a CIA agent or an agen..."

But the document ends there, and Mr. Helms's answer is missing.

A J.F.K. Assassination Glossary: Key Figures and Theories

BY DANIEL VICTOR | OCT. 26, 2017

AS THE LONGTIME government explanation goes: President John F. Kennedy was assassinated on Nov. 22, 1963, by a lone gunman, Lee Harvey Oswald. Mr. Oswald fired three bullets from a nearby building, striking Mr. Kennedy and Gov. John B. Connally Jr. of Texas.

But much of the public has never fully bought that explanation. A trove of files expected to be released on Thursday, which the federal government had long fought to keep from public view, was likely to address some of the conspiracy theories that have lingered for decades.

As you dive into the documents or read news coverage, refresh your memory here on some of the people, theories and other aspects of the assassination.

THE ZAPRUDER FILM

A 26-second home video by Abraham Zapruder is the clearest recording available of the moment Mr. Kennedy was shot. It has been pored over every which way, in hopes of finding the slightest of clues.

The film is now too brittle to run through a projector, but in 1999, the government paid Mr. Zapruder's heirs $16 million for it.

THE WARREN COMMISSION AND THE 'MAGIC BULLET'

On Sept. 27, 1964, government investigators released an 888-page report on the assassination, forming the official explanation of the events. It concluded that Lee Harvey Oswald acted alone in killing the president, and that Jack Ruby acted alone in killing Mr. Oswald two days later. It placed no blame on suggested conspirators like communists, foreign governments, the American intelligence community or right-wing conservatives.

Among its more controversial contentions was that a single bullet — derisively referred to as a "magic bullet" — struck both Mr. Kennedy and Mr. Connally, who survived the shooting. The theory was crafted in part by Arlen Specter, the longtime Pennsylvania senator who, at the time, was early in his career.

LEE HARVEY OSWALD

Mr. Oswald, a former Marine, fired three shots from the nearby Texas School Book Depository, the Warren Commission concluded. He denied that he had shot the president, calling himself a "patsy."

He was arrested hours later after shooting a police officer and ducking into the nearby Texas Theatre, the Warren Commission concluded.

JACK RUBY

Two days after the presidential assassination, Mr. Oswald was being transferred from a city jail to a county jail when Mr. Ruby stepped out from a crowd and shot him at close range, as millions of people watched on live television.

He died in jail in 1967.

SECOND SHOOTER, GRASSY KNOLL AND THE 'MAGIC BULLET'

Americans have long expressed skepticism over the official explanation that Mr. Oswald and Mr. Ruby had each acted alone. A recent poll by FiveThirtyEight and SurveyMonkey found that 33 percent of Americans believed one person was solely responsible for the assassination, while 61 percent believe others were involved.

A New York Times/CBS News Poll in 1988 found 13 percent of Americans believed Mr. Oswald acted alone.

Skeptics often say it would have been impossible for Mr. Oswald to fire fast enough to hit both Mr. Kennedy and Mr. Connally, or for the same "magic bullet" to strike both men. (Mr. Connally said he thought he was struck by a separate bullet.)

The proposed explanation would be a second shooter on what has become known as the "grassy knoll," an area ahead and to the right of the motorcade.

UMBRELLA MAN

It was a beautiful day in Dallas, not a cloud in the sky. So why was one man holding up an umbrella?

The man, who can be seen in the Zapruder film and in other images, became the object of fascination. Could he have been signaling messages to gunmen? Was his umbrella rigged with some kind of weapon?

Josiah Thompson, a researcher, gave the mysterious figure a name that would stick: Umbrella Man.

"The only person under any umbrella in all of Dallas, standing right at the location where all the shots come into the limousine," he said in a 2011 New York Times short documentary by Errol Morris. "Can anyone come up with a non-sinister explanation for this? Hmm? Hmm?"

As it turns out, Umbrella Man could. Louie Steven Witt came forward and testified in Washington in 1978, explaining that his umbrella was meant to protest the Nazi-appeasement policies of Joseph P. Kennedy, the president's father. The elder Kennedy supported the British Prime Minister Neville Chamberlain, who often carried an umbrella as an accessory, and he hoped the president would get the message.

MEXICO CITY

Mr. Oswald visited Mexico City for six days shortly before the assassination. He said he was there to obtain visas from the Cuban and Soviet Union embassies.

But some people suspect Mr. Oswald worked with other people there to plan the attack, and his exact actions during his time there remain mysterious. Experts think the documents released on Thursday could focus on meetings he had there.

Who's Fueling Conspiracy Whisperers' Falsehoods?

ESSAY | BY CLYDE HABERMAN | APRIL 30, 2017

ITALIANS HAVE A WORD for it: dietrologia.

Pronounced dee-EH-tro-lo-GEE-ah, it derives from the word for "behind." It is the study of what lurks behind everything — dietro. For many Italians, truth is rarely so careless as to lie on the surface, especially in public affairs. Someone or something must be manipulating events, unseen, as if from behind a curtain.

English is not graced with a single word to express that concept. Behindology doesn't quite cut it. But the idea exists all the same. Most succinctly, we call it conspiracy theory, and it has long been with us. But not until now have Americans had a president who may reasonably be described as their conspiracy theorist in chief.

For years, Donald J. Trump carried the torch of "birtherism," the baseless premise that President Barack Obama was born outside the United States. In the presidential campaign last year, Mr. Trump claimed to have witnessed what somehow no one else managed to see: thousands of Muslims in New Jersey cheering the devastation of Sept. 11, 2001. Ascension to the nation's highest office has not changed him in this regard. Without offering any evidence, he has insisted, for example, that Mr. Obama wiretapped his telephones and that millions of noncitizens voted illegally for Hillary Clinton.

Retro Report, a series of video documentaries that revisit major news stories of the past to demonstrate their continued relevance, looks at the present state of dietrologia all'americana by re-examining the granddaddy of modern conspiracy speculation: Who killed President John F. Kennedy? It has long been clear that many Americans, perhaps most, do not accept the official verdict that Lee Harvey Oswald acted alone in Dallas on Nov. 22, 1963.

"There's nothing quite like the Kennedy assassination, I think, in the realm of conspiracy theory," Alexandra Zapruder told Retro Report.

Ms. Zapruder is uniquely positioned. Her family and Kennedy's death, as she chronicled in a recent book, have been inextricably linked ever since her grandfather, a clothing manufacturer named Abraham Zapruder, captured the fatal scene with his 8-millimeter Bell & Howell Zoomatic camera.

The Zapruder film, a total of 486 frames lasting 26.6 seconds, was not the only visual record of the murder. Home movies providing insights were also taken by other witnesses, Orville Nix and Marie Muchmore. But Mr. Zapruder, who died in 1970, happened to be standing at a spot on the motorcade route where he was able to film the horror in full. The passage of more than half a century has not diminished the shock power of his footage.

From almost the moment the shots were fired, conspiracy theories flourished: Oswald did not act alone, or was not involved at all. A plot to kill Kennedy was hatched by the Mafia. Or it was by the Central Intelligence Agency. Or by Cubans. Or by Texas oilmen. Or by various Democrats, not least of them the man who was elevated to the presidency, Lyndon B. Johnson. One hypothesis held that the real target was John B. Connally, the Texas governor who was riding in the car with Kennedy.

During the 2016 campaign, Mr. Trump chimed in with a characteristically vague and unsubstantiated suggestion that Senator Ted Cruz's father, a Cuban immigrant, had a connection to the killing.

The Kennedy assassination was a watershed moment, when public faith in government and other pillars of American civic life began to come undone. The unraveling is well underway, with conspiracy theories in full bloom.

Retro Report examines a particularly incendiary one of recent vintage: the outlandish assertion that Mrs. Clinton was behind a pedophile ring operating out of a Washington pizza parlor. Except for the existence of that pizzeria, nothing about this story bears a resemblance to reality. It should be laughable. Yet some take it seriously. One deluded man went to the parlor with an assault rifle so he could, as he put it, "self-investigate." He was arrested and later pleaded guilty to weapons and assault charges.

Little has deterred American dealers in dietrologia, like Alex Jones and Mike Cernovich. They and others vent paranoia on radio and in social media. And they have followers who are willing believers in shadowy intrigue: the Sept. 11 terrorist attacks were an inside job hatched by the Bush administration; the 2012 massacre at Sandy Hook Elementary School in Connecticut was a hoax. Last year a major candidate for a seat on Texas' powerful State Board of Education drew national attention for having posted a smorgasbord of conspiracies on Facebook, including a claim that Mr. Obama was a male prostitute in his youth. (She lost the race.)

Trafficking in schemes is not uniquely American. Health workers seeking to vaccinate children against polio have been killed in Pakistan by militants who detect an anti-Muslim plot. The sudden death of Pope John Paul I in 1978, a mere 33 days into his reign, spurred conspiracy theories that endure. In some Arab societies, it is standard procedure to blame the Mossad, Israel's intelligence service, for pretty much every calamity.

Still, the phenomenon has flowered in the United States. Death is notably fertile ground for conspiracy whisperers, like those who insist the Clintons killed their friend Vincent Foster and those who hint at foul play in the death last year of Justice Antonin Scalia of the Supreme Court.

Suspicion is ever-lurking now. This is a far cry from 1963 America. Opinion polls show a steep decline in public faith in institutions like the news media, academia, corporate boards, Wall Street banking houses and, for sure, the government. During his campaign, Mr. Trump capitalized on the distrust, and inflamed it, with ominous they're-out-to-get-you warnings. The entire system is "rigged," he said again and again.

Of course, modern tools of communication make it possible to spread falsehoods with lightning speed. A line often attributed to Mark Twain held that a lie can travel halfway around the world before the truth can get its boots on. With today's technology, the lie can make it all the way to Neptune and back.

Twain himself had a dietrologia turn of mind. A line in his "Tom Sawyer's Conspiracy" easily holds up amid present-day realities. What makes a successful scheme? Not truth or decency, that's for sure. "Right hasn't got anything to do with it," Tom says. "The wronger a conspiracy is, the better it is."

In Donald Trump, Conspiracy Fans Find a Campaign to Believe In

BY CAMPBELL ROBERTSON | OCT. 17, 2016

KENNER, LA. — "What the government tells you is rarely the truth, and it's never the complete truth," proclaimed Roger Stone, the veteran political operative and longtime confidant of Donald J. Trump.

To the approving hoots of several dozen audience members on Sunday in a conference room at the Crowne Plaza New Orleans Airport Hotel, Mr. Stone went on to contend that his candidate was no tool of the elite power brokers at the Trilateral Commission or the Bilderberg meetings — and then he asserted paternity cover-ups within the Clinton family, declared that one group supporting Hillary Clinton was a "criminal-based money-laundering operation" and promised "devastating" revelations among hacked emails yet to be released.

And, in a brief detour, he explained that Lyndon B. Johnson helped orchestrate the assassination of John F. Kennedy.

The last part, while hardly the focus of Mr. Stone's speech, was what had brought him, for the second year in a row, to the annual Lee Harvey Oswald Conference, a gathering of conspiracy amateurs and prolific authors that is timed around Oswald's birthday (Oct. 18). The conference is dedicated to the proposition, as the conference organizer explained in his introductory remarks, that "Lee Harvey Oswald was a patsy and that it was a coup d'état that happened and we lost our country."

At a time when talk of having lost the country is very much in vogue, along with deep suspicions of a powerful and secretive elite, the symposium seemed remarkably of the moment.

In between the dissections of events from 53 years ago, the proceedings repeatedly came back to the current election. Mr. Trump, the Republican nominee, who for years raised doubts about whether President Obama was born in the United States, has charged that

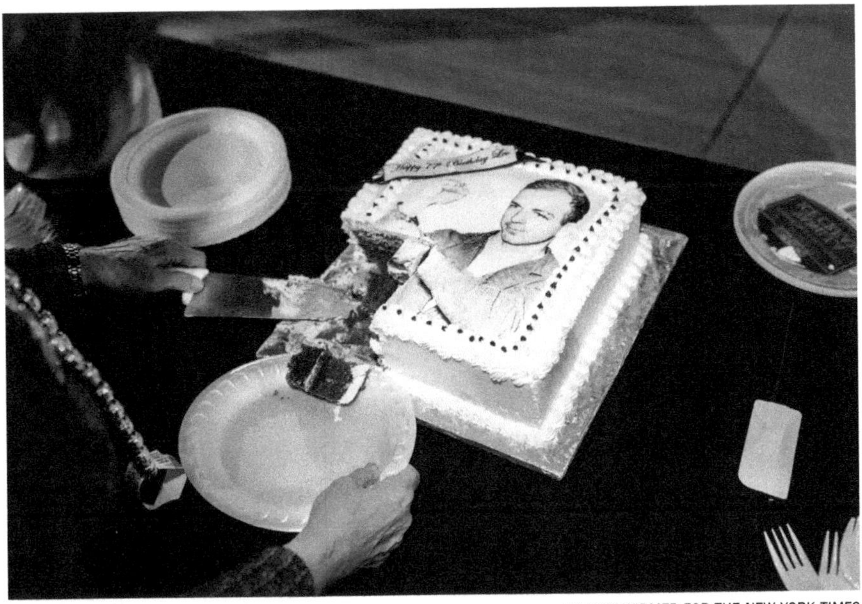

WILLIAM WIDMER FOR THE NEW YORK TIMES

Judyth Vary Baker cutting a birthday cake on Saturday during the Lee Harvey Oswald Conference outside New Orleans. The annual conference is held around Oswald's birthday, Oct. 18. Ms. Baker claims to have been his girlfriend.

the election is "one big fix" and has accused Mrs. Clinton of meeting secretly with global financial powers "to plot the destruction of U.S. sovereignty," all while intelligence officials warn of covert Russian attempts to manipulate the vote.

The idea that political figures are at the whim of shadowy forces is a core principle of the conference. The notion that elections have always been rigged was echoed by at least one presenter: Sean Stone, the son of the director Oliver Stone, whose 1991 film "JFK" is effectively one of the conference's founding documents. There was also extensive and generally favorable discussion of claims put forward by Mr. Trump that Senator Ted Cruz's father had played a role in a conspiracy behind the Kennedy assassination.

But the Oswald conference is not easy to classify politically. If there was any "party" loyalty, it was with Oswald, considered an honorable patriot manipulated and impugned by conspirators, and with Kennedy, described by one attendee as among the country's great conservatives and by one speaker as a "kind of better-looking Bernie Sanders."

Kris Millegan, an amiable publisher of conspiracy books and the chief organizer of the conference — and a self-described "Bernie man" — said the politics here flouted the usual labels.

"When you get people from the far left and far right, they're really kind of saying the same things," he said.

Still, he acknowledged, some of the things they are saying have been embraced by the Trump campaign. Trust in the government began falling shortly after the assassination, surveys show, and has never been as high since. Although trust in the mass media was high in the mid-1970s, it recently reached its lowest point in decades. A sense that some vital national essence was lost on Nov. 22, 1963, was alluded to again and again at the conference. There was also a conviction that the forces that had taken it away were still in control.

"If they did that to us 50-some-odd years ago, what are they doing today?" asked the Rev. Hy McEnery, 65, a New Orleans chaplain and a committed Trump supporter who also had questions about whether the BP oil spill had been planned.

In the beer garden of a biker bar on Saturday night, a celebration of Oswald's birthday included a cake, a "Happy Birthday" singalong and live music performed by Saint John Hunt, a son of E. Howard Hunt, one of the Richard M. Nixon operatives implicated in the Watergate break-in.

Sitting at a picnic table, George Noory considered the political landscape. A star guest at the conference, Mr. Noory hosts a popular wee-hours radio show, "Coast to Coast AM," on which government-funded dark sorcery and attempts by the military to hide evidence of an ancient race of giants are considered alongside stories that may have once seemed wildly improbable but come straight from the nightly news. Mr. Noory had on a guest last week to discuss Russia's suspected role in the hacking of the Democratic National Committee.

“What we’ve been talking about for 14 years plus, about conspiracies, about the unknown, it’s proven us to be right,” Mr. Noory said. “These things are real, and they are happening.”

To some at the conference, there was little to do about this but despair. The books on sale depicted forces aligned against the truth on an almost incomprehensible scale, arguing that the public was being duped about the Kennedy assassination, Watergate, the Sept. 11 attacks, the origin of H.I.V. and AIDS, the Nuremberg trials, the Federal Reserve, vaccinations, U.F.O.s and countless other matters. The idea that a vote for any candidate would make a difference, several said wearily, just seemed naïve.

But Mr. Stone’s brash confidence convinced others that this election was a chance to fight back — and when internet connectivity in the conference room suddenly dropped out during Mr. Stone’s speech, they saw it as a sign that someone saw Mr. Trump as a threat who had to be suppressed.

Mr. Stone finished his remarks to a somewhat divided audience — some members muttering their disagreement and others roaring with approval — and then began signing copies of his book on the secrets of the Bush family.

A man approached and raised the topic of Justice Antonin Scalia’s death in February. It seemed terribly convenient, the man suggested, leaving the Supreme Court at a 4-to-4 ideological stalemate before a potentially close election, and he asked Mr. Stone if he thought the death might have been orchestrated.

Mr. Stone responded with uncharacteristic discretion. “I do,” he said. “But that’s just my opinion.”

CHAPTER 2

9/11 and the Truther Movement

On Sept. 11, 2001, terrorists flew airplanes into New York's World Trade Center towers in what became the deadliest incident of terrorism on American soil. In the wake of the tragedy, rumors began to circulate, suggesting that the towers could not have fallen on their own. In what became known as the "Truther" movement, conspiracy theorists suggested that the attack could have been an inside job, orchestrated by the U.S. government.

500 Conspiracy Buffs Meet to Seek the Truth of 9/11

BY ALAN FEUER | JUNE 5, 2006

CHICAGO, JUNE 4 — In the ballroom foyer of the Embassy Suites Hotel, the two-day International Education and Strategy Conference for 9/11 Truth was off to a rollicking start.

In Salon Four, there was a presentation under way on the attack in Oklahoma City, while in the room next door, the splintered factions of the movement were asked — for sake of unity — to seek a common goal.

In the foyer, there were stick-pins for sale ("More gin, less Rummy"), and in the lecture halls discussions of the melting point of steel. "It's all documented," people said. Or: "The mass media is mass deception." Or, as strangers from the Internet shook hands: "Great to meet you. Love the work."

JOE TABACCA FOR THE NEW YORK TIMES

Tonya Miller Bailey, of Indiana, in the rally at Daley Plaza on Friday that served as the conference kickoff. "We've done a lot of solid research," one participant said.

Such was the coming-out for the movement known as "9/11 Truth," a society of skeptics and scientists who believe the government was complicit in the terrorist attacks. In colleges and chat rooms on the Internet, this band of disbelievers has been trying for years to prove that 9/11 was an inside job.

Whatever one thinks of the claim that the state would plan, then execute, a scheme to murder thousands of its own, there was something to the fact that more than 500 people — from Italy to Northern California — gathered for the weekend at a major chain hotel near the runways of O'Hare International. It was, in tone, half trade show, half political convention. There were talks on the Reichstag fire and the sinking of the Battleship Maine as precedents for 9/11. There were speeches by the lawyer for James Earl Ray, who claimed that a military conspiracy killed the Rev. Dr. Martin Luther King, and by a former operative for the British secret service, MI5.

"We feel at this point we've done a lot of solid research, but the American public still is not informed," said Michael Berger, press director for 911Truth.org, which sponsored the event. "We had to come up with a disciplined approach to get it out."

Mr. Berger, 40, is typical of 9/11 Truthers — a group that, in its rank and file, includes professors, chain-saw operators, mothers, engineers, activists, used-book sellers, pizza deliverymen, college students, a former fringe candidate for United States Senate and a long-haired fellow named hummux (pronounced who-mook) who, on and off, lived in a cave for 15 years.

The former owner of a recycling plant outside St. Louis, Mr. Berger joined the movement when he grew skeptical of why the 9/11 Commission had failed, to his sense of sufficiency, to answer how the building at 7 World Trade Center collapsed like a ton of bricks. It was his "9/11 trigger," the incident that drew him in, he said. For others, it might be the fact that the air-defense network did not prevent the attacks that day, or the appearance of thousands of "puts" — or short-sell bids — on the nation's airline stocks. (The 9/11 Commission found the sales innocuous.)

Such "red flags," as they are sometimes called, were the meat and potatoes of the keynote speech on Friday night by Alex Jones, who is the William Jennings Bryan of the 9/11 band. Mr. Jones, a syndicated radio host, is known for his larynx-tearing screeds against corruption — fiery, almost preacherly, addresses in which he sweats, balls his fists and often swerves from quoting Roman history to using foul language in a single breath.

At the lectern Friday night, beside a digital projection reading "History of Government Sponsored Terrorism," Mr. Jones set forth the central tenets of 9/11 Truth: that the military command that monitors aircraft "stood down" on the day of the attacks; that President Bush addressed children in a Florida classroom instead of being whisked off to the White House; that the hijackers, despite what the authorities say, were trained at American military bases; and that the towers did not collapse because of burning fuel and weakened steel but because of a "controlled demolition" caused by pre-set bombs.

According to the group's Web site, the motive for faking a terrorist attack was to allow the administration "to instantly implement policies its members have long supported, but which were otherwise infeasible."

The controlled-demolition theory is the sine qua non of the 9/11 movement — its basic claim and, in some sense, the one upon which all others rest. It is, of course, directly contradicted by the 10,000-page investigation by the National Institute of Standards and Technology, which held that jet-fuel fires distressed the towers' structure, which eventually collapsed.

The movement's answer to that report was written by Steven E. Jones, a professor of physics at Brigham Young University and the movement's expert in the matter of collapse. Dr. Jones, unlike Alex Jones, is a soft-spoken man who lets his writing do the talking. He composed an account of the destruction of the towers (www.physics.byu.edu/research/energy/htm7.html) that holds that "pre-positioned cutter-charges" brought the buildings down.

Like a prior generation of skeptics — those who doubted, say, the Warren Commission or the government's account of the Gulf of Tonkin attack — the 9/11 Truthers are dogged, at home and in the office, by friends and family who suspect that they may, in fact, be completely nuts.

"Elvis and Area 51 — we're sort of lumped together," said Harlan Dietrich, a recent college graduate from Austin, Tex. "It's attack the messenger, not the message every time."

To get the message out, the movement has gone beyond bumper stickers and "Kumbaya" into political action.

There is a plan, Mr. Berger said, to create a fund to support candidates on a 9/11 platform. There is a plan to create a network of college campus groups. There is a plan by the British delegation (such as it is, so far) to get members of Parliament to watch "Loose Change," the seminal movement DVD.

It would even seem the Truthers are not alone in believing the whole truth has not come out. A poll released last month by Zogby International found that 42 percent of all Americans believe the 9/11 Commission "concealed or refused to investigate critical evidence" in the attacks. This is in addition to the Zogby poll two years ago that found that 49 percent of New York City residents agreed with the idea that some leaders "knew in advance" that the attacks were planned and failed to act.

Beneath the weekend's screenings and symposiums on geopolitics and mass-hypnotic trance lies a tradition of questioning concentrated power, both in public and in private hands, said Mark Fenster, a law professor at the University of Florida and author of "Conspiracy Theories: Secrecy and Power in American Culture."

As for the 9/11 Truthers, they were confident enough that their theories made sense that on Friday, as a kickoff to the conference, they met in Daley Plaza for a rally (though some called it Dealey Plaza). They marched up Kinzle Street to the local affiliate of NBC where, at the plate glass windows, they chanted, "Talking heads tell lies," as the news was being read.

"I hope you don't end up dead somewhere," a companion said to a participant, hours earlier as he dropped him at the Loop. "Don't worry," the participant said. "There's too many of us for that."

2 U.S. Reports Seek to Counter Conspiracy Theories About 9/11

BY JIM DWYER | SEPT. 2, 2006

FACED WITH AN angry minority of people who believe the Sept. 11 attacks were part of a shadowy and sprawling plot run by Americans, separate reports were published this week by the State Department and a federal science agency insisting that the catastrophes were caused by hijackers who used commercial airliners as weapons.

The official narrative of the attacks has been attacked as little more than a cover story by an assortment of radio hosts, academics, amateur filmmakers and others who have spread their arguments on the Internet and cable television in America and abroad. As a motive, they suggest that the Bush administration wanted to use the attacks to justify military action in the Middle East.

Most elaborately, they propose that the collapse of the World Trade Center was actually caused by explosive charges secretly planted in the buildings, rather than by the destructive force of the airliners that thundered into the towers and set them ablaze.

The government reports and officials say the demolition argument is utterly implausible on a number of grounds. Indeed, few proponents of the explosives theory are willing to venture explanations of how daunting logistical problems would be overcome, such as planting thousands of pounds of explosives in busy office towers.

Nevertheless, federal officials say they moved to affirm the conventional history of the day because of the persistence of what they call "alternative theories." On Wednesday, the National Institute of Standards and Technology issued a seven-page study based on its earlier 10,000-page report on how and why the trade center collapsed. The full report, released a year ago, and the new study, in a question and answer format, are available online at http://wtc.nist.gov.

About a dozen researchers produced the new study over the last two months by assembling material from the longer report that addressed the conspiracy claims.

"With the fifth anniversary coming up, there seemed to be more play for the alternative viewpoints," said Michael E. Newman, a spokesman for the institute. "We have received e-mails and phone calls asking us to respond to these theories, and we felt that this fact sheet was the best means of doing so."

A nationwide poll taken earlier this summer by the Scripps Survey Research Center at Ohio University found that more than a third of those surveyed said the federal government either took part in the attacks or allowed them to happen. And 16 percent said the destruction of the trade center was aided by explosives hidden in the buildings. The survey questioned 1,010 adults by telephone and had a margin of sampling error of plus or minus four percentage points. Details are available at http://newspolls.org.

The demolition theory has managed to endure what would seem to be enormous obstacles to its practicality. Controlled demolition is done from the bottom of buildings, not the top, to take advantage of gravity, and there is little dispute that the collapse of the two towers began high in the towers, in the areas where the airplanes struck.

Moreover, a demolition project would have required the tower walls to be opened on dozens of floors, followed by the insertion of thousands of pounds of explosives, fuses and ignition mechanisms, all sneaked past the security stations, inside hundreds of feet of walls on all four faces of both buildings. Then the walls presumably would have been closed up.

All this would have had to take place without attracting the notice of any of the thousands of tenants and workers in either building; no witness has ever reported such activity. Then on the morning of Sept. 11, the demolition explosives would have had to withstand the impacts of the airplanes, since the collapse did not begin for 57 minutes in one tower, and 102 minutes in the other.

Those who believe in the demolition theory remain unpersuaded by government statements new or old, and the officials who issued the would-be rejoinders say they are not surprised. "We realize that this fact sheet won't convince those who hold to the alternative theories that our findings are sound," Mr. Newman said. "In fact, the fact sheet was never intended for them. It is for the masses who have seen or heard the alternative theory claims and want balance."

Mr. Newman was correct that the institute's reports would not convert those who favor the demolition theories, said Kevin Ryan, who is the coeditor of an online publication, www.journalof911studies.com, that has published much of the material arguing that the government's accounts are false.

"The list of answers NIST has provided is generating more questions, and more skepticism, than ever before," Mr. Ryan said.

Mr. Newman said, "NIST respects the opinions of others who do not agree with the findings in its report on the collapses of WTC1 and WTC2."

The State Department report, which officials said was written independently of the new institute study, is titled, "The Top Sept. 11 Conspiracy Theories" and says, "Numerous unfounded conspiracy theories about the Sept. 11 attacks continue to circulate, especially on the Internet." Produced by an arm of the State Department known as a "counter-misinformation team," the report is dated Aug. 28 and appears as a special feature on the department's Web site, at http://usinfo.state.gov/media/misinformation.html.

The report brought to light one little-known detail about the morning: a private demolition monitoring firm, Protec Documentation Services, had seismographs at several construction sites in Lower Manhattan and Brooklyn.

Those machines documented the tremors of the falling towers, but captured no ground vibrations before the collapses from demolition charges or bombs, according to a separate report by Brent Blanchard, the director of field operations for Protec. It is available online at www.implosionworld.com.

Asked for comment, Mr. Ryan said that his online 9/11 journal would soon publish an article on those seismic recordings. He also maintained that the Protec paper did not adequately address why puffs of smoke were seen being expelled from some of the floors. However, the federal investigators said that about 70 percent of a building's volume consists of air, and what looked like puffs of smoke were jets of air — and dust — that were pushed ahead of the collapse.

Among those now propelling the argument that explosives took down the trade center is Steven E. Jones, a physics professor at Brigham Young University, coeditor with Mr. Ryan of www.journalof911studies.com, which published his paper, "Why Indeed Did the World Trade Center Buildings Completely Collapse on 9-11-2001?"

In an e-mail message yesterday, Professor Jones did not explain how so much explosive could have been positioned in the two buildings without drawing attention. "Others are researching the maintenance activity in the buildings in the weeks prior to 9/11/2001," he wrote.

He said his investigation was finding fluorine and zinc in metal debris and dust gathered from near the trade center site, and argued that those elements should not have been found in the building compounds. "We are investigating the possibility of thermite-based arson and demolition," he wrote, referring to compounds that, under controlled circumstances, can cut through steel.

The federal investigators at the National Institute of Standards and Technology state that enormous quantities of thermite would have to be applied to the structural columns to damage them. Not so, said Professor Jones; he said he and others were investigating "superthermite."

Professor Jones also argues that the molten steel found in the rubble was evidence of demolition explosives because an ordinary airplane fire would not generate enough heat. He cited photographs of construction equipment removing debris that appeared to be red.

In rebuttal, Mr. Blanchard of Protec said that if there had been any molten steel in the rubble, it would have permanently damaged any excavation equipment encountering it. "As a fundamental point, if an excavator or grapple ever dug into a pile of molten steel heated to excess of 2000 degrees Fahrenheit, it would completely lose its ability to function," Mr. Blanchard wrote. "At a minimum, the hydraulics would immediately fail and its moving parts would bond together or seize up."

Inside the World of Conspiracy Theorists

REVIEW | BY JACOB HEILBRUNN | MAY 13, 2011

"AMONG THE TRUTHERS" is a remarkable book, not least because its author, Jonathan Kay, appears to have emerged with his sanity intact after immersing himself for several years in the wilder precincts of conspiracy theories about everything from President Obama's birthplace to 9/11 to vaccines. Like a modern-day Gulliver, he has traveled widely and conducted numerous interviews to map what seems like every nook and cranny of the conspiracist universe. Yet Kay, an editor and columnist at the conservative Canadian newspaper The National Post, has not written a Swiftian satire on the foibles of humanity. Rather, he sounds alarms about what he depicts as a mounting paranoia inspired by an invisible and nefarious oligarchy.

Kay usefully cautions at the outset, "Some conspiracies are very real." Nor is the conviction that secretive elites are manipulating the destiny of the world novel. On the contrary, Kay reminds us, the belief that coastal political elites, bankers and Ivy League intellectuals are conniving to victimize ordinary people has long been a staple on the fringes of American politics. Robert Welch, the founder of the John Birch Society, even claimed that Dwight Eisenhower's brother Milton was in cahoots with Moscow.

But as Kay sees it, conspiracy thinking is now experiencing a dangerous uptick in popularity. The terrorist threat has replaced the Red menace, as 9/11 had nothing less than what Kay deems a "seismic" effect on America's "collective intellect." He devotes much attention to the "truther" movement, which contends that the United States government perpetrated the terrorist attacks.

Some of Kay's most illuminating passages center not on what conspiracy theorists believe — even to dignify it with the word "theory" is probably to grant them more legitimacy than they deserve — but on why they are attracted to such tedious rubbish in the first place. He divides them into different camps, including the "cranks" and the "firebrands." Cranks are often reacting to male midlife crises — combating conspiracies, Kay says, offers a new sense of mission. Cranks, he adds, are frequently math teachers, computer scientists or investigative journalists.

A leading case, according to Kay, is David Ray Griffin, a former professor at the Claremont School of Theology who has devoted his retirement to writing no fewer than 11 books that examine each minute of the 9/11 timeline. Then there is Paul Zarembka, a professor of economics at the State University of New York, Buffalo, who has scrutinized "such arcane subjects as the price of individual airline stocks in the run-up to 9/11, and the tail numbers of the hijacked 9/11 aircraft." And Barrie Zwicker, a mainstream Canadian journalist turned truther, insisted on interviewing Kay while Kay was interviewing him, hitting buttons on a chess clock to regulate the amount of time each had.

Once upon a time such people would most likely have operated in relative anonymity. But with the emergence of the Internet, Kay says, they have established their own cult followings, along with the sense of superiority that is created by seeming to enjoy direct access to what actually makes the world tick. Kay writes: "Many true conspiracy theorists I've met don't even bother with Web surfing anymore. . . . From the very instant they first boot up their computer in the morning, their in-boxes comprise an unbroken catalog of outrage stories ideologically tailored to their pre-existing obsessions." As Kay sees it, the Enlightenment is itself at stake. His verdict could hardly be more categorical: "It is the mark of an intellectually pathologized society that intellectuals and politicians will reject their opponents' realities."

But is America really in such dire straits? Hardly. Kay's description sounds more reminiscent of Weimar Germany or other societies in a state of intellectual collapse than the habitual din and hubbub of American democracy. In concentrating so narrowly on truthers, Kay describes them superbly, but he may exaggerate their potential influence. He asserts but does not demonstrate that 9/11 "has had far-reaching social, political and psychological consequences that have yet to be fully absorbed or understood."

Then there is the problem of organization. At times, Kay's book can itself appear almost as convoluted as a conspiracy flowchart. He has a habit of hopscotching between topics and eras. It would also have been helpful had he drawn a clearer distinction between the muckraker, who exposes unpleasant truths, and the conspiracist, who weaves them into a fantastic plot aimed at deceiving the credulous.

Kay is forthright about chronicling loopiness on the right as well as the left. But he claims that the snobbish liberal media are at least partly culpable for the right's zaniness, because they don't treat its suspicions with more deference; this is special pleading. He also rehearses the chestnut that liberal intellectual skepticism has degenerated into nihilism, creating a relativistic world in which one opinion is as good as another. And he rather sweepingly writes that "modern academics tend to romanticize the conspiracy theorist."

Still, Kay ends on an admirable note. As his research progressed, he came to realize that his initial assumption that a distinct class of pathological crazies could be identified was mistaken. "This realization," he writes, "has taught me to be careful about my own ideological commitments. ... It has made me more self-aware when I bend the rules of logic in the service of ideology or partisanship." In a book that often suggests the grown-ups are not all right, it's a refreshingly mature confession.

AMONG THE TRUTHERS
A Journey Through America's Growing Conspiracist Underground
By Jonathan Kay
340 pp. Harper/HarperCollins Publishers. $27.99

JACOB HEILBRUNN is a regular contributor to the Book Review and a senior editor at The National Interest.

9/11 'Truthers' to Tone Protests Down, for a Day

BY COREY KILGANNON | SEPT. 9, 2011

"NO BULLHORNING during the memorial."

That's always been the rule of thumb among "truther" demonstrators at ground zero on Sept. 11, out of respect for relatives of victims of the terror attack, said Mike Skuthan, 32, a Web designer from Long Island who attends the demonstrations every year.

But after this Sunday's memorial, Mr. Skuthan said, the bullhorns and signs will again be brought out and the groups will walk from one location to another in Manhattan chanting their message and engaging passers-by to help them call for a new investigation into the attacks.

"You have the usual chants — '9-11 Truth Ends Wars,' or 'Two planes, three buildings,' " Mr. Skuthan said. "The popular one this year will probably be, 'Ten years, no justice.' "

Members of the so-called 9-11 Truth movement range from extreme conspiracy theorists who believe that the Bush administration engineered the attacks to consolidate power, roll back civil liberties and help oil mogul friends. But then there are more moderate factions that simply insist that top government officials know more about the attacks than they have acknowledged, and then used the attacks as a pretext for invading Iraq. A large percentage of activists outline — often in great detail — what they call inconsistencies in government explanations of the attacks, which many call a governmental cover-up.

There are scores of somber memorial events on Sunday commemorating the 10th anniversary of the 2001 attacks — poignant prayer services, candlelight vigils and, of course, the official commemoration at ground zero.

But for conspiracy theorists, the day's poignancy is mixed with a renewed urgency to their demand for answers, and to dispute official explanations of the attacks. The slew of events leading up to Sunday

BENJAMIN NORMAN FOR THE NEW YORK TIMES

John Williamsburg from Niles, Ohio, chats by protest signs.

include screenings of Sept. 11-conspiracy films, and widespread "street action" protests. There are discussions by the leading proponents of so-called 9/11-truth theories, and even a spiritual service led by religious leaders who believe the public has not been told the whole truth about the attacks.

Because this is the 10th anniversary, and it falls on a weekend, "truthers" are hoping to get their highest turnout ever for demonstrations, said Mr. Skuthan, who pitched in this year by making a popular Web site for "truther" events this weekend, including the locations of numerous "street actions."

The demonstrations may be more subdued this year, said Luke Rudkowski, 25, a journalist from Brooklyn.

Mr. Rudkowski is no shrinking violet. Armed with a video camera and a YouTube account, he has confronted the likes of Vice President Joseph R. Biden Jr.; Larry A. Silverstein, the leaseholder on the Trade Center; and Thomas H. Kean, a former governor of New

Jersey who was chairman of the federal Sept. 11 commission.

In 2009, Mr. Rudkowski was arrested while attempting to question Mayor Michael R. Bloomberg about the lack of health care for emergency responders.

But when Mr. Rudkowski gathers with other activists at ground zero on Sunday morning near the official, private memorial service, he says, he will be in nonconfrontational mode.

Other activists agreed that Sunday calls for a subdued approach.

"We are not going to be talking about the politics of what our organization believes," said the Rev. Ian Alterman, an evangelical minister from Manhattan and a member of Religious Leaders for 9/11 Truth, which is holding a special memorial service on Saturday at Judson Memorial Church in Greenwich Village. Mr. Alterman said his group believed that there were still many unanswered questions about the attacks, and contradictory facts — and that spiritual leaders were doing "a disservice to those who died if they do not do as

BENJAMIN NORMAN FOR THE NEW YORK TIMES

A meeting at a cafe in Greenwich Village on Thursday night of people who have alternate views of what happened on 9/11.

almost every faith traditions instructs, and seek the truth."

The service on Saturday will include prayer, song and sermons, and would include relatives of victims — but it will not include politics or speeches.

"It's a respectful memorial event, about solace," Mr. Alterman said. "No matter what side of the politics you're on, all of us have feelings of grief, and seek closure. I've asked attendees who are more politically minded not to interfere. I told them, 'Talk to me on the 12th, not on 11th. We're focusing on people here, not politics.' "

Among the listings on groundzero2011.com is a "Forgotten Heroes" memorial service on Sunday near World Trade Center Building 7, a controversial building to many in the Sept. 11 truth movement because of questions over how and why it collapsed, in a rapid free-fall several hours after planes struck the twin towers.

That service is dedicated to emergency responders who died from ailments incurred during rescue and cleanup at ground zero after the attacks.

The groundzero2011.com site offers full services for people traveling to New York City to participate in events. Aside from a ground zero vigil on Sunday morning, there are listings for numerous "street actions" around the city, including ones near the Federal Reserve, City Hall, the Stock Exchange, Federal Hall and Police Plaza.

Richard Gage, an architect from California and the founder of Architects and Engineers for 9/11 Truth, will speak at several events on Sunday. Mr. Gage's group includes architectural and engineering professionals who believe that the World Trade Center may have collapsed because of explosives planted in the buildings, and are calling for a new investigation.

Mr. Gage said that as the 10-year commemoration approaches, "The media has its attention back on 9/11."

"So it's an important time to be disseminating the information and exposing the evidence," he added. "This anniversary gives us a unique opportunity to be seen and heard."

The Weaponization of 'Truther'

ESSAY | BY MARK LEIBOVICH | NOV. 4, 2015

WHAT DOES IT mean to be a "truther"?

We are all supposedly on journeys to truth. I had a rabbi tell me this once. And to be an agent of truth — a truth-teller — is a noble thing. We praise journalists, gadflies, investigators or even politicians that speak "truth to power" and tell "hard truths" and unearth the "inconvenient truths" that defy official narratives and alter our destinies.

But it is not flattering to be called a "truther." The term originated, as far as anyone can tell, to characterize people who embraced alternative explanations for the Sept. 11 attacks. In 2006, The New York Times published an article about a convention in Chicago — dubbed the "International Education and Strategy Conference for 9/11 Truth" — in which alternative theories about the terrorist attacks were discussed. The report, by Alan Feuer, included a neutral description of 9/11 truthers, whom he characterized as a group with a "rank and file" that included "professors, chain-saw operators, mothers, engineers, activists, used-book sellers, pizza deliverymen, college students, a former fringe candidate for United States Senate and a longhaired fellow named hummux (pronounced 'who-mook') who, on and off, lived in a cave for 15 years."

A truther stereotype was born — and mutated. Today, anyone who subscribes to or perpetuates less-mainstream or in some cases deeply offensive versions of accepted scenarios becomes susceptible to the dreaded "er" suffix. Add "er," dismiss as nuts (rinse and retweet). It suggests a position on the fringe in the same way that, say, adding "gate" signifies a scandal. So why is it good to tell the truth but bad to be a truther?

Consider a recent object lesson of supposed trutherism. It occurred a few weeks ago in the Republican presidential campaign — and of course involves Donald, the Trumper. "When you talk about George

Bush," the then-maybe-front-runner said of the 43rd president during an interview on Bloomberg TV, "I mean, say what you want, the World Trade Center came down during his time."

"Hold on," the Bloomberg anchorwoman Stephanie Ruhle said. "You can't blame George Bush for that."

And why not? "He was president, O.K.?" Trump countered. "Blame him or don't blame him, but he was president. The World Trade Center came down during his reign."

In a technical sense, Trump had truth on his side. George W. Bush was, in fact, the president on Sept. 11, 2001. (As an aside, I was struck by Trump's curiously authoritarian use of "reign" to describe the tenure of an American president.) Trump did not explicitly assign blame to Bush, or say whether he could have done anything to prevent the attacks. But by raising the matter of blame, Trump was defying yet another truth that Republicans had until that point held to be self-evident: that W. held no culpability for anything that happened on 9/11.

There was an often-cited warning in the President's Daily Brief from August 2001 cautioning that Osama bin Laden was "determined to strike in U.S." But the general inclination, at least among Republicans, has been to cut Bush slack on this and credit him with "keeping America safe." Trump's remark had Bush's defenders firing up their umbrage machines. "How pathetic for @realdonaldtrump to criticize the president for 9/11," Jeb Bush tweeted. "We were attacked & my brother kept us safe." Ari Fleischer, a Bush White House press secretary, took it further, breaking out the heavy er-tillery, telling CNN: "When Trump implies that since 9/11 took place on Bush's watch he is partially responsible for it, he's starting to sound like a truther," he said. "And after all, does Donald Trump also think since Pearl Harbor happened on F.D.R.'s watch that F.D.R. is responsible?"

Trump has always been more associated with "birthers" than "truthers." "Birther," of course, is the common "er" reserved for those who believe that President Obama's birth certificate might be fake, that he was born outside the United States and that his presidency is therefore not legitimate. Trump was a vocal proponent of this view in the 2012 presidential campaign, which he made many loud noises about joining but ultimately did not. His apparent fixation on the cause was enough for many to consign him to the nativist fringe of the Republican Party, or so it seemed. It also contributed enough doubt that it compelled Obama to actually release his long-form birth certificate at a White House news conference in 2011.

Trump has largely avoided discussing the Obama birth-certificate issue in this campaign. He is an avowed nonfan of the word "birther," which he told Politico in 2012 was "a derogatory term, created by a certain group in the media" (he instead called it Obama's "place-of-birth issue"). But to this point, trutherism in its original 9/11 sense has never really been Trump's thing. Fleischer told me that he intentionally used the word "truther" as an epithet. In a sense, he was counterpunching in a classically Trumpian style — floating a notion and letting it hang there to absorb sinister connotations. Trump "did what people who want to hang dirty innuendos do, which is Donald Trump style," Fleischer said. "He made the allegation that Bush was somehow to blame, without saying how or why." Fleischer said that Trump did a similar thing recently when he brought up Ben Carson's Seventh-day Adventist faith and discussed it in a way that suggested he was confused. "I just don't know" about Seventh-day Adventists, Trump said, leaving an information vacuum for sinister thoughts to flourish.

Trump, Fleischer said, was inviting listeners to conflate legitimate questions of Bush's handling of pre-9/11 intelligence with more easily dismissed (or screwball) notions. "I'm not going to give Donald Trump the benefit of the doubt about anything he leaves unsaid," he told me. Fleischer is unaligned in the Republican primary race and says he is not a truther or a birther or any kind of "er" except for a "Fleischer" — which he says could refer to someone (like himself) who does not believe recent studies equating the consumption of certain red meats with an increased risk of cancer. "I don't buy the bacon stories," Fleischer said. "That means I'm a Fleischer." Or a "Flesher."

It's difficult to pinpoint exactly when "truther" became so readily weaponized. In debates about previous conspiracy theories, no one used terms like, say, "Kennedy assassination truther." No one dismissed as "Elvis truthers" those who believed that Elvis Presley remained alive. A recent Rawstory.com headline identified Rage Against the Machine's bassist, Tim Commerford, as a "moon-landing truther," although no one would have used such a term at the time of the actual — or alleged — moon landing.

But after that 2006 Times article, truthers were suddenly everywhere. Subsequent reports — in The Washington Post, Vanity Fair and U.S. News & World Report — all made reference to 9/11 "truthers," although it took a while for the word to acquire its full-on wacko connotation. In recent years, "truther" has come to have its own totally discrete constellation of evolving meanings and history. Social media, as it tends to do, has accelerated the process.

After NASA recently reported that scientists had found signs of water on Mars, some skeptics dismissed the news as concocted, in the words of Rush Limbaugh, to "help advance their left-wing agenda on this planet." Newsweek presented these counterarguments under the headline "Mars Conspiracy 'Truthers' React to NASA's Water Announcement." Vice recently profiled a "drought truther" who maintained that the catastrophic lack of rain in California was caused by "a secret weather-control operation orchestrated by the Powers That Be, part of a doomed attempt by government geoengineers to stop global warming." "Stevie Wonder truthers" have questioned whether the singer is in fact blind or is just faking it (for some reason). The foremost Wonder truther, Bomani Jones of ESPN, cited as evidence a guy who claimed to have sold Wonder three TVs. Jones later acknowledged to me, in an interview for this magazine, that his Wonder trutherism was "a somewhat inappropriate joke that has taken on a life of its own."

You can't help wondering how many sectors of trutherism begin similarly — goofs that spin out of control, to a point at which they are taken quasi-seriously. The Internet is a supercollider of alternative interpretations — if not realities — and the people who embrace them. People then marginalize those views by calling perpetrators truthers. Things can get very pitched in short order. Every topic — Benghazi, droughts and Mars — becomes a potential battlefield between information and misinformation, truth and truthers.

Trutherism can quickly become stranger than fiction, whatever is which. It becomes a thing, if not a meme. Our individual journeys to truth play out via search engine. You long for a less-networked, less-noisy and less-dismissive community of believers versus skeptics. Or at least I do. Is it me or did conspiracy theorizing and mythmaking used to be so much more fun? I miss the Sasquatch and Area 51 people. "The truth is out there," as the U.F.O. buffs used to say. And they used to be "buffs," not "truthers," in those days of greater innocence and less dismissiveness, before the truthers were out there, too.

CHAPTER 3

Conspiracies on the Right

In the lead-up to the 2016 presidential election, conspiracy theories begun by far-right activists left the fringe and began to show up in mainstream reports. These conspiracies largely revolved around the Clintons, dogging Hillary Clinton's health, her aides and her supposed involvement in a child sex ring run out of a Washington, D.C., pizzeria. The articles in this chapter speak to the depth that these conspiracies have reached in contemporary politics and how they transitioned from the right-wing media to the center stage.

Did You Hear the Latest About Hillary?

OPINION | BY ZEYNEP TUFEKCI | SEPT. 12, 2016

HILLARY CLINTON HAS pneumonia. Did you know she has a body double? She was that blond woman waving at reporters in front of Chelsea Clinton's apartment a few hours after Mrs. Clinton felt unwell and left the Sept. 11 commemoration at ground zero.

Did you also hear that Mrs. Clinton has Parkinson's disease? Her coughing fits prove it, as does her latest bout of illness. She has epilepsy, as well as advancing dementia. She has managed to hide all these illnesses through almost a year and a half of a grueling campaign because the man the world thinks is the head of her Secret Service detail is actually her hypnotist. He's also a medical doctor.

No, I haven't lost my mind. I've just lost many hours on social media, where these conspiracy theories run rampant.

Well before Mrs. Clinton fell ill and had to be assisted into a van on Sunday, former Mayor Rudolph W. Giuliani of New York, a supporter of Donald J. Trump, said on Fox News that the news media had failed to cover her health and that viewers should "go online and put down 'Hillary Clinton illness,' take a look at the videos for yourself."

The events of last weekend will not help Mrs. Clinton, who spent Monday at home and canceled a trip to California. Nor will they help the rest of us, stuck in this conspiracy election.

Yes, the Clinton campaign should have disclosed her pneumonia diagnosis on Friday, curtailed her schedule and allowed her to recover. Lack of disclosure only increases the number of people who suspect she's hiding something.

But there's also no amount of disclosure that would change the minds of people who think she's been hiding epilepsy, Parkinson's and dementia, thanks to her secret hypnotist and persuasive body double.

The problem is much bigger than a single moment, or this particular campaign. Conspiracy theories are like mosquitoes that thrive in swamps of low-trust societies, weak institutions, secretive elites and technology that allows theories unanchored from truth to spread rapidly. Swatting them one at a time is mostly futile: The real answer is draining the swamps.

I'm originally from Turkey, so I'm used to my Western friends snickering at the prevalence of conspiracy theories in the Middle East. It is frustrating, but the reason for these theories is not a mystery. Elites do practice excessive secrecy. Foreign powers have meddled in the region for decades. Institutions that are supposed to be trusted intermediaries, separating facts from fiction while also challenging the powerful, are few and weak. It makes sense to gravitate toward explanations that attribute everything to secret cabals.

And now, with social media, what remained of controls on keeping the worst stuff out of the public sphere has been demolished.

Wait, what part of the world was I writing about again?

My coughing fit brought about by my own advanced dementia must have confused me again.

Conspiracy theories have been around a long time, but thanks to new technologies and decline of trust in institutions, it's getting worse.

First of all: There are actual conspiracies in the world. The powerful do routinely collude to hide information. To add to this, people like stories, and conspiracy theories are a form of storytelling. The trouble here isn't a healthy suspicion of power, but the transformation of a culture of political distrust into a swirl of bizarre tales divorced from facts.

We expect traditional news outlets to act as gatekeepers for information, helping us distinguish truth from rumor. They've never been perfect at this job, but the precarious economics of the industry is making the situation even worse. The new, internet-driven financing model for news outlets is great for spreading conspiracy theories. Each story lives or dies by how much attention it attracts. This rewards the outrageous, which can get clicks more easily.

However, conspiracy theories can live only to the degree they can find communities to flourish in. That's where social media comes in. Finding a community online has been great for many people — the dissident in Egypt, the gay teenager in a conservative town — but the internet is not Thor's hammer, which only the purest of heart can pick up. Connecting online also works for an anti-vaccination parent or a Sept. 11 truther. Conspiracists can organize online and can push their version of the world into the mainstream.

To fight conspiracy theories, we also don't just need more fact-checkers. We need to fix the underlying dynamics.

People think that their governments are working against them, or at least not for them, and in some cases this is true. Ruling elites around the world are circling their wagons, and fueling more suspicion and mistrust. Reversing that would be the best defense against baseless paranoia that masquerades as political action.

The predominant internet business model isn't always great for democracy, but it's not the only option. We should support subscription, donation and philanthropy funded sources of information. Once "go viral or die" isn't the only game in town, and with a more transparent and responsive government, our conspiracy fever might break.

ZEYNEP TUFEKCI is an associate professor at the University of North Carolina School of Information and Library Science and a contributing opinion writer.

Man Motivated by 'Pizzagate' Conspiracy Theory Arrested in Washington Gunfire

BY ERIC LIPTON | DEC. 5, 2016

WASHINGTON — A man fired a rifle on Sunday inside a Washington pizza restaurant that has been subjected to harassment based on false stories tying it to child abuse, the police said. No one was hurt, and the man was arrested.

The man, Edgar M. Welch, 28, of Salisbury, N.C., told the police that he had come to the restaurant, Comet Ping Pong, in northwest Washington, to "self-investigate" what is being called Pizzagate, an online conspiracy theory asserting, with no evidence, that the restaurant is somehow tied to a child abuse ring. He entered the restaurant shortly before 3 p.m. with a rifle and fired it at least once inside, the police said.

The gunfire sharply escalated what had already been a tense period for the restaurant, its employees and the quiet neighborhood since the fake stories began spreading. Dozens of threats against employees had been made via email and social media.

People inside the restaurant fled, and the police locked down the area, ordering patrons of a nearby bookstore and cafe called Politics and Prose to remain locked inside. Officers with rifles and protective gear surrounded the restaurant and apprehended Mr. Welch. Two additional firearms were found, one on Mr. Welch and the other in his vehicle, the police said.

The police closed down a normally busy Connecticut Avenue, which runs in front of the restaurant, for several hours Sunday as they searched the area for other potential threats.

In a statement, Comet Ping Pong's owner, James Alefantis, condemned the people who had been spreading the bogus stories about child abuse.

"What happened today demonstrates that promoting false and reckless conspiracy theories comes with consequences," he said. "I hope that those involved in fanning these flames will take a moment to contemplate what happened here today and stop promoting these falsehoods right away."

Bradley Graham, co-owner of Politics and Prose, said the incident was a worrisome event during an uneasy time for the neighborhood. "This is one of the things we feared," Mr. Graham said as the police surrounded his bookstore with rifles and weapons drawn. "That this could go from a social media attack to something much more dangerous and physical."

Mr. Graham said he and others had been disappointed that the local law enforcement authorities had not previously responded more aggressively to try to stop the harassment related to the fake claims, particularly after one supporter of the Pizzagate theory shot a live video from within the restaurant during a busy dinner shift.

The misinformation campaign about Comet began when the email account of John D. Podesta, an aide to Hillary Clinton, was hacked and his emails were published by WikiLeaks during the presidential campaign. Days before the election, users on the online message board 4chan noticed that one of Mr. Podesta's leaked emails contained communications with James Alefantis, Comet's owner, discussing a fundraiser for Mrs. Clinton.

Sabrina Ousmaal, owner of a French restaurant called Terasol, which is across the street from Comet, said that other businesses in the area had also been targeted by threats and that the response from the authorities so far had been insufficient.

"The F.B.I. and the police were notified repeatedly of these death threats and calls, emails, online posts," she wrote in an email Sunday, after the rifle blast. "Nothing was done. I am appalled and horrified. Do people need to die for something to be done?"

CECILIA KANG contributed reporting.

How the Murder of a D.N.C. Staff Member Fueled Conspiracy Theories

BY JONAH ENGEL BROMWICH | MAY 17, 2017

THE MURDER LAST JULY of an employee of the Democratic National Committee received renewed attention from news media outlets on the right this week when a private investigator and longtime Fox News contributor said that there was "tangible evidence" that the employee, Seth Rich, had contacted WikiLeaks before his death.

The investigator has since given shifting and contradictory accounts to other news organizations, and Mr. Rich's family has grown increasingly distressed, calling the politicization of his death "painful" and "debilitating" and asking for retractions and apologies from the Fox outlets that promoted the investigator's story.

WHAT DO WE KNOW ABOUT MR. RICH'S MURDER?

Seth Conrad Rich, 27, worked for the committee for a little more than a year. He was shot in the back in July near his home in the Bloomingdale neighborhood of Washington, D.C.

Mr. Rich's murder is still under investigation by Washington's Metropolitan Police Department.

The police in Washington responded to the sound of gunshots early in the morning of July 10 and found Mr. Rich, who was still conscious, at an intersection in Northwest Washington near his house. Mr. Rich was taken to a hospital, where he died a little more than an hour later.

A spokesman for Mr. Rich's family, Brad Bauman, said Mr. Rich had been on a long walk after returning from a bar and was talking with his girlfriend on the phone at the time of his death.

He said the family believes that Mr. Rich may have been murdered during a failed robbery attempt; his watch strap was damaged, but his wallet and other possessions were still on him.

WHAT ARE THE ALLEGATIONS BEING MADE ABOUT MR. RICH'S MURDER?

In an August interview, Julian Assange, the founder of WikiLeaks, discussed Mr. Rich's death, and hinted that he had shared material with WikiLeaks.

"Whistle-blowers go to significant efforts to get us material and often very significant risks," Mr. Assange said in the interview, with a Dutch television station. "There's a 27-year-old who works for the D.N.C., who was shot in the back, murdered, just two weeks ago, for unknown reasons as he was walking down the street in Washington."

Pressed by the host to be more direct, Mr. Assange said, "I'm suggesting that our sources take risks and they become concerned to see things occurring like that."

He would not answer when asked directly whether Mr. Rich was a source, but he said that WikiLeaks was investigating what he called a "concerning situation." Later, WikiLeaks offered a $20,000 reward for information about Mr. Rich's murder.

In January, American intelligence officials released a report showing their belief that a Russian military intelligence unit had given WikiLeaks access to stolen material from the Democratic National Committee in an effort to influence the election, something that Mr. Assange has consistently denied.

Mr. Assange's comments about Mr. Rich have allowed some to spin an alternative narrative, in which Mr. Rich was the source of the leaked emails. No credible evidence has emerged, however, that Mr. Rich was in contact with WikiLeaks.

WHAT HAPPENED THIS WEEK?

On Monday, Rod Wheeler, a Washington private investigator who was hired by the Rich family to look into the death of their son, suggested in an interview with a Fox station in Washington that there was "tangible evidence" that Mr. Rich had communicated with WikiLeaks before his death.

On Tuesday afternoon, CNN reported that Mr. Wheeler had said in an interview he had "no evidence" that Mr. Rich had contacted WikiLeaks and that he had "only learned about the possible existence of such evidence" through a reporter at Fox News.

The Metropolitan Police Department issued a statement on Tuesday saying that "the assertions put forward by Mr. Wheeler are unfounded."

Later on Tuesday, Mr. Wheeler, who was a Washington police officer from 1990 to 1995, repeated his allegations in an interview with Sean Hannity on Fox News on Tuesday night. He told Mr. Hannity that he had talked to a federal investigator who said he had seen Mr. Rich's case file.

But in that interview, Mr. Wheeler clarified that he had never seen such emails directly, nor was he willing to say definitively to Mr. Hannity that Mr. Rich had emailed WikiLeaks, though he concluded that "it sure appears that way."

"Is there any evidence that he might have been disgruntled by the treatment of Bernie Sanders and the unfairness and that the fix was in to put Hillary in that position and maybe he had evidence of that?" Mr. Hannity asked of Mr. Rich. Mr. Wheeler said that he had not found any.

Mr. Wheeler, who has made outlandish comments on the air in the past, did not respond to emails and return phone calls on Wednesday requesting clarification of his account.

WHAT IS THE FAMILY SAYING?

The Rich family regrets hiring Mr. Wheeler and has objected to his many public comments.

Mr. Bauman, a communications professional who often represents Democratic causes and has worked as a pro bono spokesman for the family since last summer, said Wednesday afternoon that the family was asking that Fox News and the Fox affiliate retract their reports and apologize for damaging their son's legacy.

Mr. Bauman said that the Riches had retained Mr. Wheeler on the advice of Ed Butowsky, a Dallas businessman and conservative commentator who offered to pay for the investigator's services.

Aaron Rich, Mr. Rich's brother, said in an email Wednesday that Mr. Wheeler had "discredited himself as an objective investigator" and had lost the confidence of the family. He said that the politicization of his brother's death had been "painful" and "debilitating."

"Why everyone feels the need to use his death for their own motives is beyond us," he wrote. "We simply want to find his killers and grieve. Instead, we are stuck having to constantly fight against non-facts, baseless allegations, and general stupidity to defend my brother's name and legacy."

He continued, "This only prevents us from moving forward in our grieving and distracts from answering the only question that matters — Who murdered my brother and my parents' son, Seth?"

The Demented Detectives on Seth Rich's Case

OPINION | BY ANNA MERLAN | MAY 26, 2017

SETH RICH DIED on the night of July 10, 2016. The conspiracy theories were born days later. The process by which these baseless theories about his death snaked from Reddit to Twitter to Fox News illustrates just how thin the membrane has become between the conspiracy world and the mainstream.

Police say that Mr. Rich, a 27-year-old on the staff of the Democratic National Committee, most likely died in a botched robbery. But by July 13, alternate explanations emerged: A site called WhatDoesItMean.com claimed he was on his way to the F.B.I. to testify against Hillary Clinton.

Conspiracy theories help people who feel politically disempowered respond to a perceived loss of control. So it made sense, when Mrs. Clinton's win seemed assured, that supporters of both Donald Trump and Bernie Sanders were convinced that Mr. Rich's death showed ruthless corruption in the Democratic Party.

Conspiracy theories have been widespread among Americans for years, but they found particular prominence in the 2016 election because many people felt locked out of the process and distrustful of the news media. Mr. Trump, who repeatedly said that the press was dishonest and that the election would be "rigged" against him, fed and fed off this attitude.

But the Rich theories wouldn't have gone beyond WhatDoesItMean.com and Reddit without the help of prominent backers. In August, Julian Assange insinuated that Mr. Rich could have been the source of the D.N.C. emails put out by WikiLeaks and offered a $20,000 reward for information on Mr. Rich's death, despite the fact that a hacking persona going by Guccifer 2.0 claimed responsibility. Mr. Assange says that WikiLeaks doesn't reveal its sources, but if Mr. Rich leaked the emails, he would be able to distance himself from accusations that he'd acted as a funnel for a Russian intelligence operation.

This is how the modern conspiracy ecosystem works. Theories are hijacked by the self-interested. Mr. Assange was trying to protect his reputation. For others, the motive is financial. Alex Jones, the founder of Infowars, claims fluoride is put in the water supply to control people — and then sells a Fluoride Shield supplement. Often the motives are partisan: Both Pizzagate and Spirit Cooking — wild theories that accused Democratic insiders of engaging in satanic rituals and child sex abuse — were shared by right-wing outlets like Drudge Report and The Washington Times to discredit Democrats.

Mr. Assange's insinuations broke a dam: Before long, private "investigators" emerged, offering their dubious help to the Rich family. A Republican lobbyist named Jack Burkman offered more reward money, walking through Washington neighborhoods with posters reading, "Do you know who murdered Seth Rich?"

That pattern of attention-seekers attaching themselves to the case repeated itself again and again. Robbin Young, a former Playboy model who's claimed to be in contact with Guccifer 2.0, has implied that she fears being killed as a result of her own "investigating." Mike Cernovich, a far-right blogger, has also gotten involved. Even the Russian embassy in London tweeted "#WikiLeaks informer Seth Rich murdered in US but MSM was so busy accusing Russian hackers to take notice."

The biggest fish in this foul pond, though, is Sean Hannity of Fox News, who recently latched onto the Rich story, promoting it on his popular prime-time show and on social media. Mr. Hannity, a fierce Trump partisan, seemed aware that his speculation about Mr. Rich's death could deflect attention away from the multitude of disasters dogging the White House and at his own scandal-plagued network. And he surely knew that the story would play well with his audience, which was eager to see the news about the Trump team's Russia connections as a mainstream media smoke screen and Mr. Rich's murder as the real fire.

MICHAEL ROBINSON CHAVEZ/THE WASHINGTON POST/GETTY IMAGES

Mary Rich, the mother of Seth Rich, at a news conference last year.

After vigorous public shaming — including a Washington Post op-ed essay by Mr. Rich's parents — and pressure from his show's advertisers, Mr. Hannity announced that he would stop discussing the murder ("for now," he added). Fox even retracted a story from its website. He's still tweeting, though, pledging that he's close to finding "the truth."

But the theories aren't going away. Mr. Rich's death has now become lodged firmly in the conspiracy firmament. Infowars proclaimed that Mr. Rich was a victim of the "deep state," using his death as proof that the swamp is so murky that even Mr. Trump can't drain it. And devotees of Pizzagate have written that they believe that the resolution of the Rich case will help explain a grand unified theory of diabolical government misdeeds. The demented detectives won't stop.

The ceaseless churn of increasingly unhinged theories — and Fox News's willingness to put them on air — torments the Rich family.

"It is a travesty that you would prompt false conspiracy theories and other people's agendas," Aaron Rich, Seth's brother, wrote in a letter to Mr. Hannity's producers, "rather than work with the family to learn the truth."

ANNA MERLAN, an investigative reporter for Gizmodo Media Group, is writing a book about conspiracy theories.

Sean Hannity, a Murder and Why Fake News Endures

COLUMN | BY JIM RUTENBERG | MAY 24, 2017

IF WE CAN LEARN anything from the latest triple-bank-shot of a conspiracy theory coursing through the alt-reality media — this one involving the unsolved murder of a Democratic National Committee staff member named Seth Rich — it's this: Fake news dies hard.

God knows people have tried. In the last few months, journalists, academics, technology experts, civic-minded foundations and well-intentioned politicos have devoted decades of collective brain hours to an all-hands effort to stanch the conspiracy theories and outright falsehoods roiling our democracy.

Facebook and Google have worked up new computer formulas and dispatched dedicated teams of humans to push the corrosive stuff off their platforms or, at the very least, to let readers know when something doesn't look right. Ad makers are pulling their advertising from sites that run false items. And educators are working up "news literacy" programs to teach students how to tell the difference between real, corroborated journalism and naked lies dressed in the colors of veracity.

But as the Seth Rich story shows, we're going to need a bigger algorithm.

In case you haven't been following it, the Seth Rich conspiracy holds that before his death (or, in this version of events, assassination) in July Mr. Rich had been involved in the leaking of Clinton campaign emails to WikiLeaks, which the United States intelligence community has attributed to Russian-sponsored hackers.

You can see the partisan appeal. If you don't want to believe American intelligence assessments that the Russians were behind the breach — supposedly to help the electoral prospects of President Trump — and if you don't like all the news about the investigations into the Trump campaign's ties to Russia, well, there's an alternative fact set to grab onto: Mr. Rich did it and paid for it with his life.

The problem, of course, is that there's no real evidence for the notion.

The police in Washington have theorized that a thief may have killed Mr. Rich in a botched robbery attempt.

The Rich story has been kicking around since July, but flared anew last week, when FoxNews.com and the Fox affiliate in Washington, WTTG, quoted an investigator working with the Rich family as saying that Mr. Rich had been in contact with WikiLeaks before his death.

But when questioned by Oliver Darcy of CNN, the investigator acknowledged that, in fact, he had no evidence to suggest any such thing, and that he was only repeating what the FoxNews.com reporter who interviewed him about the case had told him. (Ed Butowsky, a Dallas businessman who criticized Hillary Clinton last year, acknowledged to CNN that he helped connect the investigator with the Rich family after initially denying it to NBC.)

Still, the story lived on as a meme flowing through conservative media, which seemed to relish the chance to change the subject from the torrent of news spilling forth last week on the president's Russia troubles.

After calls from Mr. Rich's family to retract its article, FoxNews.com did so on Tuesday, saying in a statement that it had not gone through "the high degree of editorial scrutiny we require for all our reporting." It removed the article from its site.

But if you thought that would chasten people pushing the story and lead them to drop it, think again.

Tuesday afternoon Sean Hannity, who had been perpetrating the Rich conspiracy theory on his nightly Fox News show, said on his radio program, "I am not Fox.com or FoxNews.com. I retracted nothing."

Something — like a reminder that he is under lucrative contract — must have changed in the hours that followed because Mr. Hannity said on his prime-time show on Fox that he would not be "discussing the matter at this time" out of "respect for the family's wishes." Astute listeners picked up on two other words in his statement: "For now."

Like water, conspiracy theories find their own level. So, where Fox News issued its retraction, The International Business Times put up a Facebook post that carried the headline, "BREAKING: Kim Dotcom claims he has evidence that proves murdered DNC staffer Seth Rich was involved in the WikiLeaks hack."

The article explained that Kim Dotcom is "a New Zealand hacker" — wanted in the United States on racketeering charges, which he denies — and the sum total of the report was that he was making a "claim." It didn't include anything about what the details might be, though the hacker said he would be happy to share those with investigators.

The unspecified claim was also picked up by the Gateway Pundit (now credentialed by the White House) and the conspiracy site InfoWars, whose Washington bureau chief, Jerome Corsi, has a long history of spreading corrosive conspiracies. You might know him from his first big breakout hit, "Unfit for Command," the book of which he was a co-author that formed the basis of the false attack against Senator John Kerry's Vietnam War record during the 2004 presidential campaign. Millennials may be more familiar with his more recent, anti-Obama "work," like "Where's the Birth Certificate?" ("Right here," Mr. Obama had answered.)

Those were books, and by today's standards, they may as well have been stone tablets. Actually, as The Financial Times recently noted, the false reportage dates to at least the propaganda war between Mark Antony and Octavian — fought in the century before the birth of Christ, communicated through coins. Coins became the printed page, which became the political advertisement, which became the cable "news" segment, the blog post, the Twitter message and the Facebook post.

So what is new is the speed of the internet and the especially fertile soil of our angry political divide.

Take heart, there are optimists. Brad Bauman, a spokesman for the Rich family (who is open about his work as a liberal political consultant), said in an interview that the developments of this week, capped by Fox News's retraction, "should not just serve as a cautionary tale but it should also serve as a message that in the end, truth does prevail. But we need to be vigilant."

And Alan C. Miller, the founder of the News Literacy Project, which teaches middle- and high-school students how to "sort fact from fiction in the digital age," said the developments of the last year had spurred many more converts to the cause he began pursuing nearly 10 years ago.

"All the viral rumors, conspiracy theories and hoaxes were a wake-up call for at least some people, and certainly some institutions that are now moving to address this, including news organizations, social media organizations and educational institutions," he told me.

But no matter what the media ecosystem does to stop uncorroborated conspiracies and false information, they will continue to live on as long as there are people eager to spread it and viewers and readers eager to believe it. All the algorithms in the world can't stop that.

JIM RUTENBERG writes the Mediator column for The New York Times.

The Conspiracy Theory That Says Trump Is a Genius

OPINION | BY MICHELLE GOLDBERG | APRIL 6, 2018

LAST WEEK ROSEANNE BARR — who, with the hit reboot of her show, has become one of the most prominent Donald Trump supporters in the country — tweeted that the president has freed hundreds of children a month from sexual bondage. "He has broken up trafficking rings in high places everywhere," she wrote. (The tweet has since been deleted.)

Barr's tweet, puzzling to the casual observer, was a reference to QAnon, an expansive, complicated pro-Trump conspiracy theory. The theory is fascinating as an artifact of our current political derangement, but more than that, it's profoundly revealing about the lengths to which some Trump supporters will go to convince themselves that his presidency is going well.

As Paris Martineau explained in New York Magazine, QAnon was born last October, when someone claiming to have "Q" level security clearance started a cryptic thread on 4chan, the online message board and troll playground. It was titled, "The Calm Before the Storm," a phrase Trump had recently used. Q posted hints, some in the form of questions, ostensibly meant to help clued-in Trump supporters understand what was really going on in Washington beneath the facade of chaos and incompetence. ("What is military intelligence? Why go around the 3 letter agencies?")

From these clues, a sprawling community on message boards, YouTube videos and Twitter accounts has elaborated an enormous, ever-mutating fantasy narrative about the Trump presidency. In the QAnon reality, Trump only pretended to collude with Russia in order to create a pretext for the hiring of Robert Mueller, the special counsel, who is actually working with Trump to take down an inconceivably evil and powerful network of coup-plotters and child sex traffickers that includes Hillary Clinton, Barack Obama and George Soros.

AL DRAGO FOR THE NEW YORK TIMES

"QAnon points out that this is the beginning of the end for the Clintons," said Jerome Corsi — a prominent proponent of the lie that Obama was born in Kenya — on a YouTube broadcast in January. He warned that the world would be forced to contend with "films of innocent children pleading for their lives while people are butchering them." Once that happens, presumably, Trump will be revealed as a master of 12-dimensional chess who successfully distracted smirking elites with his buffoonery while he was quietly saving the world.

Posts on other websites, as well as YouTube videos, Twitter accounts and even a book, have taken the theory in countless directions, encompassing characters from the model Chrissy Teigen to disgraced politician Anthony Weiner. The creativity poured into QAnon is striking; it's like something between a sprawling work of crowdsourced postmodern fiction and an immersive role-playing game.

But for many people, QAnon is very real. Barr has tried to make contact with Q on Twitter. InfoWars, the website run by conspiracy theorist Alex Jones — who has a close relationship with Trump confidant Roger Stone — has consistently promoted it. Last month, Cheryl Sullenger, senior vice president of the anti-abortion group Operation Rescue, posted an article on the group's website about an "intel drop" from Q revealing a White House plan to end Planned Parenthood. Sean Hannity retweeted a post with the #QAnon hashtag.

Some elements of the QAnon conspiracy theory — secret elites, kidnapped children — are classic, even archetypical. "In all Western culture, you can argue that all conspiracy theories, no matter how diverse, come from the idea of the Jews abducting children," Chip Berlet, the co-author of "Right-Wing Populism in America: Too Close for Comfort," told me. Stories about globalists stealing children for sex aren't that far removed from stories about Jews stealing children to use their blood making matzo.

One twist, however, makes QAnon unusual. Conspiracy theories are usually about evil cabals manipulating world events. QAnon, by contrast, is a conspiracy theory in which the good guys — in this case, Trump and his allies — are in charge. It's a dream of power rather than a bitter alibi for victimhood. It seems designed to cope with the cognitive dissonance caused by the gap between Trump as his faithful followers like to imagine him, and Trump as he is.

On Thursday, the usually even-keeled Mike Allen published a piece in Axios titled, "The case for extreme worry," about how those close to Trump are panicked by his erraticism. The president's whims and resentments have led to stock market convulsions and may soon result in painful tariffs that affect American farmers, an important part of his base. Mueller's special counsel investigation continues to close in. Republicans have lost special election seats in red-leaning areas all over the country. But QAnon offers assurance that everything is under control.

Barr, for example, retweeted a QAnon post arguing that conservative criticism of the omnibus spending bill, legislation many on the right deplored, was shortsighted. In releasing funds to the military, it said, the bill would set off a climactic series of events: "Swamp drain begins, military seizes TRILLIONS in cabal assets, returning them to the people." An inspector general report would then reveal the establishment's unspeakable crimes, after which "the strings will be cut from the propaganda machine and people will stop falling for the garbage MSM," or mainstream media. Trump, and those who believe in him, would be vindicated.

You don't create a wild fantasy about your leader being a covert genius unless you understand that to most people, he looks like something quite different. You don't need an occult story about how your side is secretly winning if it's actually winning. Publicly, many right-wing politicians and pundits disdain the Mueller investigation and pretend to believe that Trump's ties to Russia are negligible. But among part of the Trump base, the effort to explain them away appears to be creating psychic strain.

"You cannot possibly imagine the size of this," said a Q dispatch last month. "Trust the plan. Trust there are more good than bad." Q almost certainly doesn't know any state secrets, but he, she, or they understand that some fervent Trump supporters require more reassurance than they're willing to admit. Their desperate conviction that they will be proven right about Trump betrays a secret fear that they will be proven wrong.

MICHELLE GOLDBERG is an Op-Ed columnist for The New York Times.

What Is QAnon: Explaining the Internet Conspiracy Theory That Showed Up at a Trump Rally

BY JUSTIN BANK, LIAM STACK AND DANIEL VICTOR | AUG. 1, 2018

Do you remember Pizzagate? It's a little like that: a web of baseless conspiracy theories. And its supporters were highly visible at an event for the president in Florida.

THOSE WATCHING PRESIDENT Trump's rally in Tampa on Tuesday couldn't help but be exposed to a fringe movement that discusses several loosely connected and vaguely defined — and baseless — conspiracy theories.

In one shot on Fox News, the president was partially obscured by a sign in the crowd reading "We Are Q." In another shot during the president's speech, a sign promoting the debunked Seth Rich conspiracy theory, with the hashtag #Qanon, came into focus in the center of the screen. Some attendees wore T-shirts with a blocky Q. Others held up signs with the letter.

They were all self-described "followers of Q," an anonymous person or group of people who claim to be privy to government secrets. That supposedly classified information has been revealed on the 4chan and 8chan message boards and spread around mainstream internet platforms like YouTube, Facebook and Twitter. Q has attracted people — the exact number is hard to know — eager to consume his "bread crumbs," or new details in a sprawling web of conspiracy theories.

What is going on?

JUST GIVE ME THE BASICS SO I CAN MINIMALLY UNDERSTAND WHAT'S GOING ON

Here is the short version: Q claims to be a government insider exposing an entrenched, international bureaucracy that is secretly plotting all sorts of nefarious schemes against the Trump administration and its supporters. The character uses lingo that implies that he or she has a military or intelligence background.

It's a stew of various, but connecting, conspiracy theories that generally hold Mr. Trump as a conquistador battling a cabal of anti-American saboteurs who have taken over government, industry, media and various other institutions of public life in a plan to ... well, the overarching goals of the nefarious actors are not clear.

THE SLIGHTLY LONGER VERSION

A growing group of people (more on the scale and scope of that community below) are coalescing around a collection of theories and half-thoughts that they believe reveal an untold story of current world events. To decode what they believe is actually happening, followers of Q sift through the president's tweets, government data sets or news articles.

Ben Decker, a research fellow at the Shorenstein Center on Media, Politics and Public Policy at Harvard, described followers of the QAnon narrative as "an interactive conspiracy community."

Sometimes followers of Q just look for signs that he exists. A popular Rosetta Stone they use is to look for uses of the number 17 (the letter Q's placement in the alphabet). So when Alabama's football team presented Mr. Trump with a jersey with the number 17, it was taken as coded signaling of Q's influence. (The team was visiting the White House as the champions of the 2017 college football season and had presented President Barack Obama with a jersey bearing the number 15 when it visited after winning a championship in 2015.)

Q's followers ascribe secret coordination and hidden motives to an endless parade of politicians, journalists, and leaders of industry and other institutions. Often, their theories are wildly at odds with reality.

The community uses the language of mind-bending pop culture alternate realities like "The Matrix" or "Alice in Wonderland." It is common to tell stories of how followers have been "redpilled," or have come to believe that observable reality is false and the QAnon narrative is real.

The shared rush to interpret clues from a "drop" of information from Q resembles something close to what video gamers call an MMO, or massive multiplayer online game.

WHY SHOULD I CARE ABOUT A FRINGE CORNER OF THE INTERNET?

Because QAnon is not limited to a fringe corner of the internet. In addition to its front-and-center presence at Mr. Trump's rally, it has been promoted by celebrities including Roseanne Barr and Curt Schilling, the former baseball star who has a podcast for Breitbart.

The paranoid worldview has crossed over from the internet into the real world several times in recent months. On more than one occasion, people believed to be followers of QAnon have shown up — sometimes with weapons — in places that the character told them were somehow connected to anti-Trump conspiracies.

"The biggest danger is you are one mentally unstable person away from the next massive incident that defines whatever happens next," Mr. Decker said. "The next Pizzagate, which for better or worse did define the political conversation for a while."

In June, a man armed with a rifle and a handgun drove an armored vehicle to the Hoover Dam on what he said was a mission from QAnon: to demand that the government release the Justice Department's report from its inspector general on the conduct of F.B.I. agents during the investigation into Hillary Clinton's use of a private email server.

The report had actually been released the day before, but Q's followers believed there was a secret, second report that contained far more damning information about the F.B.I. There is no indication that such a report exists. The man was arrested after a standoff with the police.

Most recently, a suspicious and possibly armed man showed up at the law offices of Michael Avenatti, the lawyer for Stephanie Clifford, the adult film performer known as Stormy Daniels, after Q posted a link to Mr. Avenatti's website and a picture of the office building. The man did not enter the premises.

In an interview, Mr. Avenatti said he had received a large number of threatening emails and social media posts in recent months, "but this one we have significant reason to believe posed a significant threat." He said local law enforcement was investigating the incident.

"I do think it is dangerous, absolutely," Mr. Avenatti said. "And I think it is incumbent upon the president to quash this nonsense as opposed to feeding it."

Mr. Decker said the prominence of QAnon T-shirts and signs at Mr. Trump's televised rally in Tampa, and the elevation of that imagery via cable news coverage of the rally, were troubling. "In a sense, the internet won," he said.

"These are communities craving attention, they're craving media appearances, they're craving exposure so they can further propagate," he said. "It is very concerning to exponentially increase the audience of this content to eight-, nine- or 10-figure populations."

WHAT ELSE CAN WE SAY ABOUT THE SIZE AND SCOPE OF THIS COMMUNITY?

The /r/GreatAwakening subreddit board vibrantly shares memes with 49,000 followers, making it a medium-size board. There are Facebook groups, one of the most popular of which has nearly 40,000 members sharing hundreds of posts with one another a day.

Video explainers of Q followers talking through potential connected topics have racked up millions of views on YouTube, and the numbers of tweets out there are too numerous to count (and the difficulty in discerning genuine posts versus bot activity makes Twitter a poor measuring stick anyway).

But perhaps the greatest signal of the sustained, dedicated audience for this discussion can be found in the seismic traffic to websites and apps set up to collect and curate preferred 4chan posts about Q.

In April 2018, an app called "QDrops" was among the 10 most downloaded paid iOS apps in the Apple Store, according to an NBC report that cited an analytics site.

The Qanon.pub site was created in March 2018 and has quickly established an audience of over seven million visits a month, according to the web analytics company SimilarWeb.

JUSTIN BANK is a senior editor for internet and audience. He was previously a senior editor at The Washington Post.

LIAM STACK is a political reporter. Before joining the politics team, he was a general assignment reporter based in New York and a Middle East correspondent based in Cairo.

DANIEL VICTOR is a Hong Kong-based reporter, covering a wide variety of stories with a focus on breaking news. He joined The Times in 2012 from ProPublica.

A Trail of 'Bread Crumbs,' Leading Conspiracy Theorists Into the Wilderness

ESSAY | BY MATTATHIAS SCHWARTZ | SEPT. 11, 2018

GO HUNGRY FOR too long, and a lot of strange things will start to look like food. The smallest morsels become precious, especially if you believe they form some kind of trail with a meal at the end. This is true not only of physical sustenance; it is true of knowledge as well. You always find scattered crumbs — inscrutable analogies, esoteric equations, unverified allegations from anonymous sources — gathered around those questions about which we know the least.

For months now, one such anonymous source — an internet user called "Q Clearance Patriot" or "Q," posting on anarchic, underbelly-of-the-internet message boards like 4chan and 8chan — has been spreading its "crumbs" across the web, offering up a running commentary on the state of the nation in a gnomic and paranoid style. To call the result a mere "conspiracy theory" doesn't quite do it justice, shortchanging both its utterly absurd wrongness and its vast pseudo-explanatory power. Q's prophecies are something closer to a grand unifying conspiracy theory, one that incorporates older absurd theories (stretching back to the Kennedy administration) and continuously spins off new tendrils, glomming itself onto news events as they unfold. Good and evil, it claims, have mustered two warring teams; the fate of humanity hangs in the balance. The heroes are the military (especially the Marines) and President Trump, who is secretly cooperating with Robert Mueller to, some disciples imagine, uncover a global ring of sex-trafficking pedophiles. And even this risks making it sound more realistic than it is.

What's most striking about the Q phenomenon is how many people take it seriously. #QAnon billboards have started showing up beside highways in Georgia. Q's supporters have turned up en masse, with signs and T-shirts, at Trump rallies. Roseanne Barr tweets about it. In June, an armed man was arrested after blocking traffic near the Hoover Dam; in jail, he reportedly wrote a letter to Trump including Q's motto: "Where we go one, we go all." Trump shows no particular inclination to discourage the theory. In August, he posed for a picture with the former talk-radio host Michael Lebron, who promotes Q theories online, inside the Oval Office.

"Your President needs your help," writes Q in one "Q drop" — that's what Q's followers, or "bakers," call each bread crumb. Q engages the bakers as collaborators who "research" lines of inquiry and offer possible answers to Q's hypnotic flurries of leading questions. ("Las Vegas. What hotel did the 'reported' gunfire occur from? What floors specifically? Who owns the top floors?") But Q balances fear-mongering with notes of reassurance: The bakers are, by poring over each nonsensical hint, supposedly aiding their fellow "patriots" on the inside. Bad news is merely a "distraction." The president's behavior is merely a ruse. The good guys are secretly in control, and they are going to win.

So the baker-followers assemble the crumbs into what they call "dough" or "bread," to be circulated online — feverishly complex diagrams and bulletin-board collages of words and images. Bright red lines highlight connections, an approach familiar to viewers of "True Detective" or "Homeland" or "The Wire," and satirized by a popular GIF of a wild-eyed Charlie Day, from the TV comedy "It's Always Sunny in Philadelphia," standing in front of a messy bulletin board. Day's character, who is working in a corporate mailroom, has convinced himself that half of the company's employees don't exist, even as a friend assures him that not only are they real, but also that "they have been asking for their mail on a daily basis." Rather than deal with the complex reality of his duties, he has retreated into fantasy.

Whoever posts as Q postures as a government insider with a high-level "Q" security clearance and an enigmatic connection to Trump's inner circle. "I can hint and point but cannot give too many highly classified data points," Q wrote, in one of the earliest posts. A bit later: "These are crumbs and you cannot imagine the full and complete picture." To reveal too much, Q claims, would be dangerous. Repeated and prolonged exposure to the crumbs — there are more than 2,000 of them, as of early September — is, supposedly, the only path toward comprehension. "These are like our generation's 'fireside' chats," a grateful baker on Reddit wrote.

The crumbs, of course, tend not to lead anywhere. Q was wrong about the imminent arrests of prominent Democrats, wrong about John McCain using his health as "cover" to step down from the Senate, and wrong (so far) about the "storm" or "great awakening" — a national redemption, under martial law, that is perpetually hours away from happening. Still, the bakers reassure themselves by validating their beloved source, assembling what they call "proofs" — tangential connections between the bread crumbs and reality. Many of these have to do with the recurrence of certain numbers, like 17 (Q is the 17th letter) or 4, 10 and 20 (which correspond with Trump's initials). These are known as "Qincidences," and as Q often tells us, there are "no coincidences." Scattered among Q's crumbs are plenty of yeasty bits that could later be puffed up into Qincidences — hazy aerial photos, coordinates for downtown Manila, a '90s rock video, alphanumeric strings that could be codes or passwords. More likely, according to a review by one security researcher, they are the result of random typing.

Sherman Kent, a postwar official considered a founding figure of the United States intelligence community, liked to say that C.I.A. analysts are driven by three wishes: to know everything, to be believed and to have some positive impact. The bread crumb draws its power from that first wish — our human discontent with how little can actually be known. Curiosity, in other words.

The line between inquiring our way into the unknown and speculating our way into it is evident only in retrospect. We can see this most clearly at the edges of old maps, where the terrain loses all proportion before decaying into dragon-filled waters and rings of fire. But these maps were at least informed by the actual journeys of actual explorers; just as Kent's C.I.A. analysts had, for better or worse, real raw intelligence. What makes conspiracy-theory bread crumbs different is that they do little more than rearrange the known in hopes of sparking a conversation about the unknown. They speculate, interpret wildly, ask baffling questions. They adjust their narratives to link new developments back to old hints. These rhetorical moves all serve to conceal the fact that they have nothing verifiable to add.

Q is just one particularly absurd manifestation of this mode of thinking. A related tendency can be found in corners of the anti-Trump resistance, where Twitter gurus highlight whatever nuggets of the day's news are favorable to their camp. Like the bakers, some flatter themselves by calling their work "research," but their real formula is to aggregate and speculate. (If the Russian ambassador, Paul Manafort and Donald Trump were all present at the same Washington reception in April 2016, surely they must have hammered out the details of a criminal conspiracy then and there?) The president is forever on the verge of impeachment; the biggest bombshells are always just about to drop; the full perfidy of the Trump-Russia iceberg is always just below the waterline, visible only to those faithfully connecting the dots. These figures lack Q's mystique (and are far, far better connected with reality), but they share Q's vulnerability: Their influence depends on producing a nonstop stream of portentous tidbits, little pellets of encouragement to keep followers hitting the retweet button.

Q's bread crumbs are spiced with accessible citations from fairy tales and pop culture: "Alice in Wonderland," Snow White, "The Godfather." And yet Q has, thus far, refrained from mentioning the story that gave us the bread-crumb analogy in the first place — the story of Hansel and Gretel, as set down by the Brothers Grimm. It is an unusually brutal story, containing accounts of child abandonment, cannibalism and the unexplained death of the protagonists' mother. It takes place during a famine, and its core theme is hunger. Lack of food causes Hansel and Gretel's parents to abandon them, giving each a piece of bread before leading them deep into the woods.

The trail of bread crumbs left by Hansel, though, is not intended as a series of clues for someone else. It is more like Theseus' ball of thread, allowing the children to find their way back home. And this plan does not work: The crumbs are eaten by birds, and the children wander deeper into the unknown, to the witch's house. By the time they arrive, they are starving.

Q's bakers, likewise, are starving for information. Their willingness to chase bread crumbs is a symptom of ignorance and powerlessness. There may be something to their belief that the machinery of the state is inaccessible to the people. It's hard to blame them for resorting to fantasy and esotericism, after all, when accurate information about the government's current activities is so easily concealed and so woefully incomplete. Despite Q's insistence that "we are in control" and "you have the power," the truth may be even more frightening.

MATTATHIAS SCHWARTZ is a contributing writer for the magazine and a former staff writer at The New Yorker, where he won the Livingston Award for international reporting. His last feature for the magazine was about the former C.I.A. director John Brennan.

You Don't Need to Go to the Dark Web to Find Hateful Conspiracy Theories

COLUMN | BY JIM RUTENBERG | OCT. 31, 2018

YOU DON'T HAVE to go deep into the internet to find the baseless conspiracies that provided a backdrop for mass murder in Pittsburgh and the recent pipe-bomb mailings to Barack Obama, the Clintons, George Soros and CNN. They are served up in plain sight, for profit, at airport bookstores, at movie-theater chains and on cable television.

They come by way of publishing houses like Hachette and Penguin Random House; film distributors like Universal Home Studios and Lionsgate; theater chains like AMC and Cinemark; and 21st Century Fox, the parent company of Fox News.

Those companies have all helped feed a segment of the media business that should be called what it is — the Incitement Industry.

It rakes in profits by serving up agitprop that targets liberals, Democrats and "deep state" operatives who are said to be plotting to destroy America for the benefit of darker-skinned migrants or a shadowy consortium of elites.

You can see this kind of thing in the pages of "Liars, Leakers and Liberals" by the Fox News opinion host Jeanine Pirro. Published in July by Center Street, a division of the Hachette Book Group, Ms. Pirro's book lays out "the globalist, open-border oligarchy" that, the author asserts, is seeking to nullify the results of the 2016 presidential election.

"The perpetrators of this anti-American plot include, but are not limited to, the leadership at the F.B.I., the C.I.A., N.S.A. and other intelligence agencies, the Democratic Party and perhaps even the FISA courts," she writes.

"Liars, Leakers and Liberals" has spent 13 weeks on the New York Times best-seller list.

Another recent best seller in the same vein, "Resistance Is Futile!" by the conservative provocateur Ann Coulter, was published by

Sentinel, an imprint of the publishing giant Penguin Random House. It argues that the "resistance" that sprang up in the wake of President Trump's election is "nothing less than a coup." And it lights into a conveniently vague villain — "the media" — in a chapter titled "For Democracy to Live, We Must Kill the Media."

"The media's position is that they're allowed to engage in lies, deception and even illegal acts to swing an election," Ms. Coulter writes.

A similar point of view characterizes the films of Dinesh D'Souza, the polemicist who had pleaded guilty to making illegal campaign contributions in 2014, only to be pardoned by President Trump this year. Moviegoers did not have to go out of their way to catch Mr. D'Souza's most recent effort, "Death of a Nation." The film had a wide release last summer, playing in more than 1,000 theaters, including those belonging to the AMC and Cinemark chains.

The film makes the case that the Nazi platform was similar to that of today's Democratic Party. Prominent among its villains is George Soros, who was allegedly sent a pipe bomb by Cesar Sayoc Jr., who also is accused of sending similar packages to Hillary Clinton and Mr. Obama.

"The progressive Democrats are the true racists," the film's narrator intones. "They are the true fascists. They want to steal our income. They want to steal our earnings and our wealth and our freedom and our lives."

The PG-13 rated film had a box office take of roughly $6 million, which paled next to the $33 million brought in by "Obama's America," a 2012 film by Mr. D'Souza that claimed Mr. Obama, as the president, sought to destroy the United States from within to sate the "anti-Colonialism" impulses of the African father he hardly knew.

"Death of a Nation" will have a second life on the streaming platforms Amazon, iTunes and Google Play, as well as on DVD, sold at Walmart, Best Buy and other retailers. The distribution is being handled by Quality Flix and Universal Pictures Home Entertainment.

The Incitement Industry can also be a driving force at Fox News, which has lately featured guests who have asserted without evidence that Mr. Soros financed the migrant caravan making its slow way toward the southern border of the United States. Someone who shared that view was the man charged with killing 11 congregants during a hate-driven shooting rampage at the Tree of Life synagogue in Pittsburgh.

The Fox Business Network opinion show "Lou Dobbs Tonight" was the setting for two particularly glaring assertions. Mr. Dobbs played the friendly interviewer as Chris Farrell, a director of a right-wing activist group called Judicial Watch, said that "the Soros-occupied State Department" was involved in the migrant caravan. After his appearance on Mr. Dobbs's program, Fox News condemned the statement and said that Mr. Farrell would no longer appear on the network.

Another guest on "Lou Dobbs Tonight," the author Sidney Powell, likened the caravan to an "invasion" that was leading to "diseases spreading across the country that are causing polio-like paralysis of our children." In that case, Mr. Dobbs pushed back, saying, "You can't very well blame that disease on illegal immigrants."

The hysteria led Bill Kristol, the conservative Republican who was once a regular on the Rupert Murdoch-owned Fox News, to tell Brian Stelter of CNN that it was time for Fox's owners and investors to take a hard look at the rhetoric spilling out of its news channel.

And the Fox News anchor Shepard Smith, who has become something of an in-house ombudsman for the network, told his viewers on Monday, "There is no invasion. No one's coming to get you. There's nothing to worry about."

(Representatives for Fox News and its parent company, 21st Century Fox, did not comment for this article.)

There is certainly enough hyperbole to go around. Earlier this week the GQ correspondent Julia Ioffe apologized for saying on CNN that Mr. Trump had "radicalized so many more people than ISIS ever did."

Violent acts, it should be noted, are the responsibility of those who commit them, and the perpetrators have various ideological motivations. But the grist for emotionally disturbed or just plain violent people has never seemed so readily available.

"It might be fun or profitable for people to take up a megaphone against others," said James Alefantis, the owner of Comet Ping Pong in Washington, the site of the internet's "pizzagate" conspiracy. "The fact is, it takes just one individual to decide to take violent action."

Mr. Alefantis's livelihood suffered last year when a gunman — who was supposedly "investigating" the theory that the restaurant housed a Clinton-run child prostitution ring — fired an AR-15 rifle at his place of business.

Alex Jones of Infowars got rich by promoting conspiracies like that one, as The New York Times has reported. While he is in his own category, Mr. Jones got his message out to a mass audience through the tech giants YouTube, Facebook, Twitter and Apple — which eventually cut ties with him under intensifying criticism of their failure to curb the spread of misinformation. That, in turn, fed complaints among some conservatives that Silicon Valley, under pressure from liberals and the news media, was guilty of thought-policing.

But where is the line between falsehoods that may incite violence and good, old-fashioned American political hyperbole? And should book publishers and entertainment companies be more careful about the products they send out into the world in a tense sociopolitical atmosphere?

"I don't want some publisher telling me that something is beyond bounds," Mr. Kristol told me in an interview. "I'm a libertarian on points of view and even interpretations of history."

But after noting that conspiracy theories of recent vintage have whipped up fear and hatred, Mr. Kristol added, "There are things that normal fact-checking would rule out. It's not a matter of ideology; it's truth."

I asked Hachette, the company behind "Liars, Leakers and Liberals," whether Ms. Pirro's statement that Mr. Soros has "an agenda to destroy this country and the capitalist system" had passed muster with the publisher's editors and fact-checkers. I got no answer.

Sentinel, the division of Penguin Random House that published Ms. Coulter's recent best seller, was at least willing to engage. Its publisher, Adrian Zackheim, told me the author's views were "expressions of opinion."

Maybe it's time to stop labeling her book "nonfiction."

JIM RUTENBERG writes the Mediator column for The New York Times.

Wild Speculation Isn't Worth Much. A 'Theory,' However . . .

ESSAY | BY STEPHEN KEARSE | DEC. 19, 2018

YOU EXPECT, WHEN YOU encounter a new "theory," that it will make some facet of the world feel more lucid — that the inexplicable will be explained. A good theory clarifies things, aids our understanding. It's prepared for us to scrutinize and audit, testing its explanatory power. The strongest ones have been refined, continually, until the case they make is as resilient as it is persuasive.

It's strange, then, how "theory" has come to describe ideas that build no case at all.

The president, for instance, has now spent years insisting that voter fraud is a rampant and unchecked scourge. On separate occasions and for various elections, he has attributed the suspected fraud to undocumented immigrants in general, to Californians in particular and to legitimate voters registered in multiple states. These claims lack any rigorous evidence, and they rarely congeal into any kind of testable premise. Nevertheless, they have mysteriously become a "theory." A 2017 Washington Post headline said "Trump's unfounded voter fraud theory" was fueled by a conversation with a German golfer he knows (though "theory" was later changed to "story," and the golfer denied it). "Trump revives voter fraud theory without evidence," The Hill reported this April. After the 2016 election, Mother Jones noted that one man had, according to the police in Texas, tested "Trump's voter fraud theory" by trying to cast two ballots himself. But how could you test a theory that lacked any propositions? When an NBC reporter recently asked Trump for any evidence of this sprawling conspiracy, the president replied, "I don't know, you tell me."

Other theorists aren't as bashful. The so-called "prestige theory," the brainchild of a Kanye West fan named Spencer Wolff, appeared with smug enthusiasm: "The clues are right in front of us," Wolff tweeted.

Built on a shaky foundation of tweet exegesis, movie references and celebrity trivia, Wolff's theory posited that West's recent embrace of conservative politics was actually an elaborate piece of performance art. The theory had all the coherence of a stranger's dreams: Wolff's assertions were so tenuous and hedged that he couldn't even decide why West would pose as a right-leaning provocateur. "What exactly is he trying to accomplish with this performance art piece?" Wolff later wrote. "I don't know." Yet he still felt emboldened enough to call it a theory, and fans debated it accordingly.

When evidence runs particularly thin, being flexible helps. During confirmation hearings for Brett Kavanaugh, we met with what many media outlets labeled the "doppelgänger theory" — in which it was agreed that someone must have sexually assaulted Christine Blasey Ford in 1982, but it may have been a man easily confused with Kavanaugh. This idea rose to the realm of theory after being elaborated by the conservative activist and amateur detective Ed Whelan, who tweeted floor plans, yearbook photos and a neighborhood map in an attempt to build a case for Kavanaugh's innocence. His speculations were granted such credibility that Ford was asked to respond to them in her own Senate testimony.

This is what's striking about all these new theories and others like them: Their incoherence does little to stop their reception. Even as they are poked and prodded and perhaps disproved, they live and die not on their cunning but on their flat persistence. None of them look at observed facts and seek to explain their relationship; they do the opposite, starting with an unshakable conclusion (Trump is beloved, West is left-leaning, Kavanaugh is blameless) and speculating that some facts must exist to support it. And once stamped with the imprimatur of a "theory," they demand to be taken seriously, no matter how flimsy they may be.

Whatever air of authority attaches to a "theory" is a relatively recent development. Theories have circulated through mathematics, medicine and philosophy without being accorded any particular weight on their own. Charles Hutton, an 18th-century mathematician, contrasted them with application and suggested that mere theory was sometimes incomplete without practice. The 20th-century scholar John A. Scott saw theory as a ruse deployed by unlearned hacks: "They regard a theory of more importance than facts," he wrote of some of his peers, "for if they can only spin a theory they have no need of facts." Outside scholarship, theories had even less import. An 1893 Washington Post article, "The Man Who Thinks," mocked a bar patron who outlined a "theory concerning astral intoxication" — the joke being not just that the man was drunk but that he was drunk enough to think a theory might convince anyone it wasn't his doing.

At that point, though, science was still relatively disorganized and imprecise. The modern connotations of "theory" are a legacy of the industrialization and professionalism of science, with theory and practice converging in larger labs, bolder experiments, better tools. Scientists began presenting and testing theories with increasing explanatory power and empirical backing, making it possible for them to put forth more penetrating explanations of how the world worked — "generalized" explanations that Albert Einstein called "theories of principle." Their foundations, he wrote in 1920, were "not hypothetical constituents, but empirically observed general properties of phenomena, principles from which mathematical formulae are deduced of a such a kind that they apply to every case which presents itself." Such theories weren't just rigorous or extensive; they explained *everything*.

Einstein was specifically referring to theories of principle in physics, but the idea that science could produce such powerful, all-encompassing explanations appealed to scholars in a range of fields. Economists, linguists, anthropologists and even manufacturers put forth their own grand ideas, publishing unified theories of everything from surgical shock to employment. Theory gradually became the fulcrum of disciplines like literary scholarship and philosophy. Other disciplines didn't always uphold the granular empiricism of Einstein's general theory, but they tended to get the sweeping rhetoric just right. Everyone talks; theorists talk big.

What distinguishes the modern "theory" is the outsourcing of corroboration. Many seem altogether indifferent to the evidence available. Claims like the president's function as writing prompts: He provides the premise and others search for its explanation.

In calmer waters, this crowdsourcing dynamic can be a pleasant one. In online fan communities, for instance, theories are great entertainment; it's fun and enriching to pose a provocative thought like "Jack from 'Titanic' is a time traveler" and gnaw on it as a group, producing imaginative close readings of a work. Megaweird ideas, too — the theory that the parents in "The Brady Bunch" murdered each other's former spouses, or that Stevie Wonder can actually see — are absurd enough to make for amusing thought experiments.

But it's telling that the first two rules of r/FanTheories, a Reddit forum dedicated to such speculation, are "Don't be a jerk" and "Please provide evidence." Open-ended prompts don't lend themselves to dispute. How can you collectively weigh claims without knowing what the claims are or what evidence prompted them? To dig into the president's voter-fraud theories, you would have to imagine hundreds of disparate polling centers being duped on a scale decisive enough to swing elections, including legions of fraudulent voters, spoofed registrations, recruiters and managers — a staggeringly sophisticated secret cabal that decided, for some reason, to devote all its energy to losing a presidential election. What is this even a theory of? Without shared evidence or explicit reasoning, a theory is just a befuddling spectacle — spitballs taking flight.

But there's always an audience eager to keep those spitballs in the air. Before a suspect was identified in October's pipe-bomb campaign against news organizations and Trump critics, theories proliferated even as information remained scarce. The conservative pundit (and former Kanye West tutor) Candace Owens tweeted (then deleted) that they were "fake bomb threats" by leftists "going ALL OUT for midterms." The film producer and conspiracy buff Tariq Nasheed considered it "clear" that the bomber was connected to law enforcement. The right-wing vlogger Bill Mitchell had another conjecture: "Here's my theory: This 'bomb scare' is a hoax perpetrated by Democrat operatives to stop Trump from calling them a mob and blunt his rallies."

Theorists pointed to the current political climate, divisive political rhetoric, the long histories of right- and left-wing violence, the recklessness of our leaders, the looming elections. It felt as though all they were doing was pointing, offering no real interpretation. In the absence of evidence, they doubled down on their convictions and speculated about how those convictions might be confirmed. The truth was out there, they insisted: If only we would heed their theories, we could find it.

STEPHEN KEARSE is a freelance writer and critic in Washington. He has previously contributed to The Baffler, Complex and Hazlitt. He last wrote a First Words column about the strange expectations of an "ally."

CHAPTER 4

Donald Trump and the Mainstream Conspiracy Theory

Donald Trump's entanglement in conspiracy theories predates his 2016 presidential campaign. His initial forays into politics were tied to his promotion of the "birther" movement, suggesting that Barack Obama was born in Kenya and therefore invalidating his presidency. Throughout his campaign and his time in office, he has made headlines through routine references to conspiracy theories, propagated largely by right-wing extremists and individuals such as Alex Jones, owner of Infowars.

Even as He Rises, Donald Trump Entertains Conspiracy Theories

BY MAGGIE HABERMAN | FEB. 29, 2016

IT WAS A QUESTION that most major presidential candidates would have quickly dismissed as absurd, even offensive: What do you make of these theories that Justice Antonin Scalia was murdered?

For Donald J. Trump, it appeared unavoidably juicy, and possibly the next big pop-culture fixation. "You know, I just landed, and I'm hearing it's a big topic," Mr. Trump told the radio host Michael Savage from South Carolina, in an interview just a few days after the Supreme Court justice's unexpected death. Even as he said he could not speak to whether a special commission should investigate the death, he added,

"They say they found a pillow on his face, which is a pretty unusual place to find a pillow."

Mr. Trump, unlike most presidential candidates, does not shrink from addressing, and in some ways legitimizing, the wildest of hypotheticals. He has declared on a presidential debate stage that he knew a 2-year-old who immediately developed autism from a vaccination. He has appeared on the radio show of the noted conspiracy theorist Alex Jones, who has suggested that the government played a role in the Sept. 11, 2001, terrorist attacks and the 2013 Boston Marathon bombings. He has said on Twitter that President Obama might have attended Justice Scalia's funeral had it been held at a mosque, feeding into the pervasive rumor that the Christian president is actually a Muslim. And he shared with a rally crowd a dramatic story of a United States general executing Muslim insurgents with bullets dipped in pigs' blood, which has been dismissed as an Internet rumor.

Part hair-salon gossip, part purveyor of forwarded conspiracy emails, Mr. Trump has exploited the news cycles of an Internet era in which rumors explode like fireworks and often take a long time to burn out. Mr. Trump's willingness to touch on what passes for fact on fringe websites puts him in a unique class for a national major party front-runner.

"It's like a walking, talking Enquirer magazine," said Erick Erickson, the former editor in chief of the conservative website RedState, referring to the popular supermarket tabloid National Enquirer. Mr. Erickson often shut down interest in conspiracy theories on his website, such as the so-called birther rumors that Mr. Obama was born in Kenya.

Such supermarket tabloids "do very well — people do like the stories of aliens meeting with presidents," said Mr. Erickson, who has often clashed with Mr. Trump.

It is not a total surprise that Mr. Trump is the candidate most likely to use the phrase "I hear" before stating something as fact, no matter how flimsy the information he passes along. A man who reveled in his presence in the New York tabloid pages for decades, he saw firsthand the power of stories, especially those that shock people, to command attention. But the expectations for what a presidential standard-bearer would pass along have typically been higher.

It was the "birther" theories that Mr. Trump used to stoke interest in his own potential candidacy in 2011. That year, he repeatedly demanded that Mr. Obama produce his Hawaiian birth certificate. In April of that year, he claimed to have sent investigators to the state: "They can't believe what they're finding," he said, though he has never made public any such findings, and Mr. Obama later released his birth certificate.

Mr. Trump has since tried to steer clear of the birthplace claims about Mr. Obama. But he used similar questions to try to inject doubt about Senator Ted Cruz of Texas, who was born in Canada to a United States citizen.

The candidate has used Twitter to pass along other dubious theories, including false crime statistics about blacks and questions about Senator Marco Rubio's eligibility to be president. Mr. Rubio was born in the United States.

Pressed about passing along such conjecture by the ABC News host George Stephanopoulos on Feb. 21, Mr. Trump gave a response he frequently uses to deflect responsibility for sharing inaccurate information. "Somebody said he's not, and I retweeted it," Mr. Trump said. "We start a dialogue, and it's very interesting."

Mr. Trump's campaign manager, Corey Lewandowski, said his candidate was not bound by convention and looked to start conversations, not to be a mediator of topics. "The great part about the Internet is, it gives a forum for people to express their ideas, and when he sees an idea that he thinks is worthy of having a discussion about," Mr. Lewandowski said, Mr. Trump will sometimes repost things that he does not agree with.

As for what he says, Mr. Lewandowski said, "Mr. Trump is willing to have conversations and discuss issues that other candidates aren't willing to discuss because they're so politically correct."

But some of the subjects Mr. Trump has flirted with during his candidacy are darker, and more consequential, such as the mosque post about Mr. Obama and Justice Scalia's funeral, which he later insisted was meant to be a joke.

He has also promoted the notion that vaccines cause autism, a claim that has been widely debunked by doctors and scientists. "Just the other day, 2 years old, 2-and-a-half-years old, a child, a beautiful child went to have the vaccine, and came back, and a week later got a tremendous fever, got very, very sick, now is autistic," Mr. Trump said at a Republican debate in September.

When another presidential candidate, Michele Bachmann, then a Minnesota congresswoman, made a similar claim in the 2012 campaign, she was savaged by news media commentators for the remarks; Mr. Trump received little serious blowback.

And an Internet rumor around the time of the Sept. 11 attacks about Muslims in New Jersey cheering the fall of the World Trade Center towers was cited as fact by Mr. Trump, who said that "thousands" of Muslims had hailed the attacks, spurring weeks of controversy in the fall. To buttress his case, he reposted information on Twitter from the website Infowars, hosted by Mr. Jones, the conspiracy theorist.

More recently, at a South Carolina campaign event, Mr. Trump touched on the smoky theory that the identity of those who funded the attacks was still not publicly known. If he wins, he said, "you will find out who really knocked down the World Trade Center."

Christopher Ruddy, the editor in chief of the conservative website Newsmax, said Mr. Trump's popularity was driven in part by the larger mistrust of traditional institutions, including the mainstream news media.

"I'm not so sure he believes there's anything to these things, but I believe he enjoys the conversation about it; it keeps the script moving," said Mr. Ruddy, who wrote a book on the death of the former Clinton White House aide Vincent W. Foster Jr., which was ruled a suicide but remains a topic of conspiracy theories.

Mr. Trump, Mr. Ruddy said, is using a stream-of-consciousness style, speaking "as if you were the neighbor next door or a friend of his." That "we're just chatting" approach has let working-class voters see the New York plutocrat as someone to whom they can relate, Mr. Ruddy said.

And by virtue of his newness as a phenomenon, he is able to withstand what could otherwise be withering scrutiny. "It works for him, where it wouldn't work for other people," Mr. Ruddy said.

But to publicly entertain such theories, Mr. Erickson said, means sliding down a dangerous slope. "You hand yourself over the idea that there's an invisible hand at work that you can't see," he said. "You then begin to cast about to blame someone for controlling that invisible hand, and you lose perspective on what is and is not happening, and what is and isn't real."

The primary season has shown that there is little downside for candidates who stretch the truth. Whether Mr. Trump changes his approach if he becomes the party's nominee and faces millions of independent and Democratic voters remains to be seen. But for now, Mr. Trump has embraced the funhouse-mirror aspect of his party's fringe.

One of his notable media stops at the end of 2015 was a half-hour visit with Mr. Jones, on his wide-reaching radio show. Mr. Jones ended the program by thanking his guest, adding, "You will be attacked for coming on, and we know you know that."

Inside the Six Weeks Donald Trump Was a Nonstop 'Birther'

BY ASHLEY PARKER AND STEVE EDER | JULY 2, 2016

JOSEPH FARAH, a 61-year-old author, had long labored on the fringes of political life, publishing a six-part series claiming that soybeans caused homosexuality and fretting that "cultural Marxists" were plotting to destroy the country.

But in early 2011, he received the first of several calls from a Manhattan real estate developer who wanted to take one of his theories mainstream.

That developer, Donald J. Trump, told Mr. Farah that he shared his suspicion that President Obama might have been born outside the United States and that he was looking for a way to prove it.

"What can we do to get to the bottom of this?" Mr. Trump asked him. "What can we do to turn the tide?"

CHERYL SENTER FOR THE NEW YORK TIMES

Donald J. Trump in 2011 in Portsmouth, N.H., on the same day that President Obama released his long-form birth certificate after pressure from people like Mr. Trump.

Mr. Farah recalled that Mr. Trump even proposed dispatching private investigators to Hawaii, Mr. Obama's birthplace, to resolve the debate.

Mr. Trump's eagerness to embrace the so-called birther idea — long debunked, and until then confined to right-wing conspiracy theorists — foreshadowed how, just five years later, Mr. Trump would bedevil his rivals in the Republican presidential primary race and upend the political system.

In the birther movement, Mr. Trump recognized an opportunity to connect with the electorate over an issue many considered taboo: the discomfort, in some quarters of American society, with the election of the nation's first black president. He harnessed it for political gain, beginning his connection with the largely white Republican base that, in his 2016 campaign, helped clinch his party's nomination.

"The appeal of the birther issue was, 'I'm going to take this guy on, and I'm going to beat him,' " said Sam Nunberg, who was one of Mr. Trump's advisers during that period but was fired from his current campaign. "It was a great niche and wedge issue."

And starting in March 2011, when he first began to test the idea that a reality television star with no political experience could mount a campaign for the presidency, Mr. Trump could not stop talking about it.

"Why doesn't he show his birth certificate?" he asked on ABC's "The View." "I want to see his birth certificate," he told Fox News's "On the Record." And on NBC's "Today Show," he declared, "I'm starting to think that he was not born here."

The more Mr. Trump questioned the legitimacy of Mr. Obama's presidency, the better he performed in the early polls of the 2012 Republican field, springing from fifth place to a virtual tie for first.

That frenzied period culminated six weeks after it began in a surreal televised split screen between Mr. Trump and the White House briefing room, where aides released an image of the president's birth certificate proving he was born in Honolulu and Mr. Obama directly addressed the issue.

T.J. KIRKPATRICK FOR THE NEW YORK TIMES

Joseph Farah, an author and the owner of the conservative website WorldNetDaily, at his offices last month in Chantilly, Va.

It was a remarkable moment that Mr. Trump celebrated as a political victory.

Then Mr. Trump did something decidedly un-Trump-like: He dropped the issue and rarely spoke of it publicly again.

According to people apprised of the conversations, people close to him had been worried about the negative attention. Officials at NBC had also been concerned that he was alienating the large black audience of his hit show, "The Apprentice."

Indeed, damage had already been done. Some black leaders denounced him, with Jesse Jackson accusing Mr. Trump of appealing to the president's detractors with "coded and covert rhetoric for stirring up racial fears."

Several days later, Mr. Obama relished his own chance to belittle Mr. Trump with a string of taunts at the White House Correspondents' Association dinner, as Mr. Trump, seated in the audience, grew increasingly stone-faced. "But no one is happier, no one is prouder, to put this birth certificate matter to rest than the Donald," he said to laughter. "And that's because he can finally get back to focusing on the issues that matter: Like, did we fake the moon landing?"

Mr. Trump, who declined to be interviewed about the subject, was not the first to question Mr. Obama's birthplace. The narrative that Mr. Obama, whose father was Kenyan and mother American, might not meet the requirement that the president be a "natural-born citizen" first arose during his 2008 bid.

Mr. Obama's aides initially decided it was better to ignore the questions; addressing them, they reasoned, would just give them credibility.

And Mr. Trump, too, at first seemed uncertain about just how much skepticism to express over the president's place of birth. "The reason I have a little doubt, just a little, is because he grew up and nobody knew him," he said in a March 2011 interview. "The whole thing is very strange."

Yet, quickly, the world took notice. One headline referred to Mr. Trump going "Birther Lite." Another said he was a "Teeny Bit Birther." And MSNBC's "Hardball" replayed the comments, with the intro: "Let's listen to how he joins the birthers."

If Mr. Trump was offering a political trial balloon, he appeared to like the results. He started making the rounds, offering interviews on the topic and stoking public interest in the birther claims.

Mr. Trump was egged on by one key adviser — Roger J. Stone Jr., a dapper dresser and political operative known for mischief and mayhem. Mr. Stone said that he did not plant the idea with Mr. Trump, but that once Mr. Trump came to him with it, he extolled what he saw as the political upside.

"He was suspicious about it, or at least interested in it," Mr. Stone said. Among Republican base voters, he added, "many of them believe the president is foreign-born, and Trump has an ability to interject any idea that is outside of the mainstream into the mainstream."

A Gallup poll from that period showed that only 38 percent of Americans surveyed believed that Mr. Obama was "definitely" born in the United States. That number rose to 47 percent after Mr. Obama released his long-form birth certificate.

Mr. Trump also continued to reach out to Mr. Farah, founder of WorldNetDaily, a conservative website, as well as to Jerome Corsi, another conservative writer and author of "Where's the Birth Certificate? The Case That Barack Obama is Not Eligible to Be President." (The book came out shortly after Mr. Obama released his birth certificate, but shot to the top of Amazon.com's best sellers before it was even officially published.)

"He was looking for affirmation that he was on the right track," Mr. Farah said. "He was looking for a smoking gun kind of sound bite that would resonate with people."

But what most impressed Mr. Farah was just how many hours Mr. Trump was willing to devote to the question. "This was a busy guy, this was a multibillionaire, and I was surprised that he was willing to spend that kind of time on it," he said.

Mr. Farah also stressed to Mr. Trump that the issue was one of "transparency," and Mr. Trump began using the phrase.

"He started saying 'transparency,' " said Mr. Nunberg, Mr. Trump's former adviser. "It's code for, 'This guy is the Manchurian candidate.' "

Mr. Trump also said repeatedly that he had sent a team of investigators to Hawaii to unearth information about Mr. Obama's birth records. "They cannot believe what they are finding," Mr. Trump told ABC's "The View."

But as the issue exploded, people close to Mr. Trump were growing nervous.

Some people in Mr. Trump's orbit were discomfited by the line of attack, which had already been examined and rejected by many conservative news outlets. Among them was an informal political adviser, Kellyanne Conway, a Republican pollster, who cautioned that if he did run, he would need to beat Mr. Obama "on the merits."

DOUG MILLS/THE NEW YORK TIMES

President Obama made a statement in 2011 at the White House after the release of his birth certificate.

Even executives at NBC, which aired “The Apprentice,” privately called on him to tone down his remarks, fearing he would hurt ratings at a time when more than a million African-Americans tuned in every Thursday night, according to a former executive with knowledge of the discussions, speaking anonymously to share candid conversations.

The White House, too, had growing concerns. Once reserved to the fringe, the issue had now begun popping up at town-hall-style events around the country.

The turning point came in mid-April 2011, when the president delivered a major speech on the budget, only to find his remarks obscured by questions about his birth certificate.

“It was basically a message blocker that was preventing us from talking about the issues we needed to talk about because the press was chasing Donald Trump around for the next crazy thing he was going to say," said Dan Pfeiffer, the White House communications director then.

The White House counsel dispatched someone to Hawaii to find the president's original long-form birth certificate from 1961. (Years before, the president had released the "short form," an official computer-generated document that contains the information from the original.) With the document finally in hand, aides quickly scheduled a news conference.

They worried that having Mr. Obama himself release his birth certificate from the White House briefing room would undermine the dignity of the office. So they first passed out copies to reporters, and then had the president deliver remarks, in which he warned the nation about getting distracted by "sideshows and carnival barkers."

Then, almost as quickly as it began, the controversy subsided. And several weeks later, Mr. Trump decided not to seek the Republican nomination. Though he continued to do well in polls, he seemed to be more focused on his reality television pursuits.

Now, Mr. Trump almost assiduously refuses to discuss the topic, which, according to several people close to him, was always more about political performance art than ideology.

"I don't talk about that anymore," Mr. Trump told the MSNBC host Chris Matthews after a Republican debate last year.

Raising questions about the president's birth certificate — and even threatening to send a team of investigators to Hawaii — had served its purpose, raising Mr. Trump's political profile and, whether he knew it or not at the time, providing him with the rudimentary foundation upon which he built his 2016 campaign.

He even skirted close to birther innuendo after the massacre in Orlando, Fla., last month, calling into "Fox & Friends" to insinuate that Mr. Obama might sympathize with Islamic extremists. "He doesn't get it or he gets it better than anybody understands," Mr. Trump said.

But for all of his fascination with the president's birth certificate, Mr. Trump apparently never dispatched investigators or made much of an effort to find the documents.

Dr. Alvin Onaka, the Hawaii state registrar who handled queries about Mr. Obama, said recently through a spokeswoman that he had no evidence or recollection of Mr. Trump or any of his representatives ever requesting the records from the Hawaii State Department of Health.

MICHAEL M. GRYNBAUM and **MAGGIE HABERMAN** contributed reporting.
KITTY BENNETT contributed research.

Donald Trump Clung to 'Birther' Lie for Years, and Still Isn't Apologetic

ANALYSIS | BY MICHAEL BARBARO | SEPT. 16, 2016

IT WAS NOT TRUE in 2011, when Donald J. Trump mischievously began to question President Obama's birthplace aloud in television interviews. "I'm starting to think that he was not born here," he said at the time.

It was not true in 2012, when he took to Twitter to declare that "an 'extremely credible source' " had called his office to inform him that Mr. Obama's birth certificate was "a fraud."

It was not true in 2014, when Mr. Trump invited hackers to "please hack Obama's college records (destroyed?) and check 'place of birth.' "

It was never true, any of it. Mr. Obama's citizenship was never in question. No credible evidence ever suggested otherwise.

Yet it took Mr. Trump five years of dodging, winking and joking to surrender to reality, finally, on Friday, after a remarkable campaign of relentless deception that tried to undermine the legitimacy of the nation's first black president.

In fact, it took Mr. Trump much longer than that: Mr. Obama released his short-form birth certificate from the Hawaii Department of Health in 2008. Most of the world moved on.

But not Mr. Trump.

He nurtured the conspiracy like a poisonous flower, watering and feeding it with an ardor that still baffles and embarrasses many around him.

Mr. Trump called up like-minded sowers of the same corrosive rumor, asking them for advice on how to take a falsehood and make it mainstream in 2011, as he weighed his own run for the White House.

"What can we do to get to the bottom of this?" Mr. Trump asked Joseph Farah, an author who has long labored on the fringes of political life. "What can we do to turn the tide?"

What he could do — and what he did do — was talk about it, uninhibitedly, on social media, where dark rumors flourish in 140-character bursts and, inevitably, find a home with those who have no need for facts and whose suspicions can never be allayed.

And he mused about it on television, where bright lights and sparse editing ensure that millions can hear falsehoods unchallenged by fact-checking.

"Why doesn't he show his birth certificate?" Mr. Trump asked on ABC's "The View." "I want to see his birth certificate," he told Fox News's "On the Record."

And so it went.

The essential question — Why promote a lie? — may be unanswerable. Was it sport? Was it his lifelong quest to court media attention? Was it racism? Was it the cynical start of his eventual campaign for president?

It might not matter. He kept doing it, even as his most senior aides assured the public that he had long since abandoned the fallacy.

He had not. He was disingenuous until the very end, telling a Washington Post reporter just 72 hours before that he was unready to concede the president's place of birth. But he treated the weighty topic, as he does so much else, like a television cliffhanger, promising a major declaration on Friday.

And then, around 11 a.m. Friday in Washington, he gave up the lie. But he conjured up a bizarre new deception, congratulating himself for putting to rest the doubts about Mr. Obama that he had fanned since 2011. "I finished it," he declared, unapologetically. "President Obama was born in the United States — period."

Surrounded by, and in many ways shielded by, decorated veterans in his new Washington hotel, he could not resist indulging in another falsehood — that his opponent, Hillary Clinton, had started the so-called birther movement. She did not.

Much has been made of Mr. Trump's casual elasticity with the truth; he has exhausted an army of fact-checkers with his mischaracteriza-

DAMON WINTER/THE NEW YORK TIMES

Donald J. Trump in a campaign appearance on Friday at the Trump International Hotel in Washington.

tions, exaggerations and fabrications. But this lie was different from the start, an insidious, calculated calumny that sought to undo the embrace of an African-American president by the 69 million voters who elected him in 2008.

In the end, it seemed, Mr. Trump's plot to diminish Mr. Obama did not succeed. On Friday, the president of the United States seemed much bigger.

"I was pretty confident about where I was born," Mr. Obama said from the White House, a wry smile crossing his face. "I think most people were as well."

And the president had this to say about the myth heedlessly spread by the man seeking to replace him: "My hope would be that the presidential election reflects more serious issues than that."

As Donald Trump Pushes Conspiracy Theories, Right-Wing Media Gets Its Wish

POLITCAL MEMO | BY JONATHAN MARTIN | MAY 25, 2016

WASHINGTON — Ever since talk radio, cable news and the Internet emerged in the 1990s as potent political forces on the right, Republicans have used those media to attack their opponents through a now-familiar two-step.

Political operatives would secretly place damaging information with friendly media like The Drudge Report and Fox News and with radio hosts like Rush Limbaugh — and then they would work to get the same information absorbed into the mainstream media.

Candidates themselves would avoid being seen slinging mud, if possible, so as to avoid coming across as undignified or desperate.

Yet by personally broaching topics like Bill Clinton's marital indiscretions and the conspiracy theories surrounding the suicide of Vincent W. Foster Jr., a Clinton White House aide, Donald J. Trump is again defying the norms of presidential politics and fashioning his own outrageous style — one that has little use for a middleman, let alone usual ideas about dignity.

"They've reverse-engineered the way it has always worked because they now have a candidate willing to say it himself," said Danny Diaz, who was a top aide in Jeb Bush's presidential campaign. Mr. Diaz spoke with a measure of wonder about the spectacle of the party's presumptive nominee discussing Mr. Clinton's sexual escapades.

With Mr. Trump as the presumptive Republican standard-bearer, the line separating the conservative mischief makers and the party's more-buttoned-up cadre of elected officials and aides has been obliterated. Fusing what had been two separate but symbiotic forces, Mr. Trump has begun a real-life political science experiment: What happens when a major party's nominee is more provocateur than politician?

That the Republican Party has embraced someone willing to traffic in the most inflammatory of accusations comes as wish fulfillment for an element of the right that is convinced that the party lost the past two elections because its candidates were unwilling to attack President Obama forcefully enough.

In this telling, in 2008, Senator John McCain should have focused on Mr. Obama's relationships with his former pastor, the Rev. Jeremiah Wright, and the onetime radical Bill Ayers, and on discredited claims about Mr. Obama's birthplace and ties to Islam. And Mitt Romney lost four years later because he, too, ignored those issues, as well as other fixations of the conservative news media like the terrorist attack on the United States Consulate in Benghazi, Libya.

Now Republicans have a candidate who, as Mr. Limbaugh put it on his show on Tuesday, "has gone there."

"Trump has gone to all of this Clinton conspiracy stuff," Mr. Limbaugh said. Mr. Trump, he added, was "doing the job the American media and the Republican Party won't do."

The Drudge Report was downright gleeful, running a "Vince Foster Lives!" banner headline on Tuesday.

Roger J. Stone Jr., the political operative who is Mr. Trump's longtime confidant and an unapologetic stirrer of strife, called Mr. McCain and Mr. Romney "losers" for their more restrained approaches.

"Comity gets you beat," he said, adding, "It takes guts to win — and Trump doesn't look at polls, he just swings."

But that is precisely what has many Republicans, and some Democrats, nervous.

"He's never been involved in policy making or party building or the normal things a candidate would do," said Jon Seaton, a Republican strategist. "His whole frame of reference is daytime Fox News and Infowars," a website run by the conservative commentator Alex Jones.

STEPHEN CROWLEY/THE NEW YORK TIMES

Donald J. Trump on Tuesday night in Albuquerque. His unrestrained style is indisputably good TV, as his primary race opponents discovered, and poses a threat to Democrats that may not be so easily neutralized by the usual tactics.

Mark Salter, Mr. McCain's former chief of staff, said Mr. Trump was making common cause with "the lunatic fringe," citing his willingness to appear on the radio show of Mr. Jones, who has said that Michelle Obama is a man.

"I fear that it, if not a mortal blow, at least does lasting damage as the demographic clock keeps ticking away on us," Mr. Salter said of Mr. Trump's effect on the party, alluding to its dwindling base of white voters.

Mr. Salter echoed a widespread complaint, saying the news media were enabling Mr. Trump for the sake of ratings.

But Mr. Trump's style is indisputably good TV, as his primary race opponents discovered. And his asymmetrical style of political warfare poses a threat to Democrats and their likely nominee, Hillary Clinton, one that may not be so easily neutralized by the usual tactics.

Already, Mrs. Clinton's campaign is testing out different responses — juggling how much to deploy the candidate herself and how much to outsource the fiercest counterattacks. It clearly has not yet settled on the most effective approach.

"I don't think Hillary's campaign should engage in this sort of stuff," said James Carville, a Democratic strategist, referring to Mr. Trump's shift toward conspiracy-mongering. "But the pushback from surrogates and the 'super PAC' world is going to be pretty damn hard."

Anita Dunn, a former top aide to Mr. Obama, said "this is the time" for Mrs. Clinton's campaign to determine how best to respond to Mr. Trump's charges, noting that Senator Bernie Sanders of Vermont is still in the race and that Mrs. Clinton will not effectively claim the Democratic nomination until at least June 7.

But at least in the short term, Mr. Trump's willingness to hurl the most incendiary charges has given him an overwhelming advantage.

"He is winning the day," Ms. Dunn said, "if you define winning the day by dominating the coverage." She made clear that she did not.

In the next breath, though, Ms. Dunn wryly braced for more incoming. Half-jokingly imagining Mr. Trump dredging up the 1993 federal raid on the Branch Davidian compound in Waco, Tex., she said, "We haven't heard 'David Koresh' yet."

Drawing a Line From Alternative Theories to Untruths

COLUMN | BY JIM DWYER | FEB. 7, 2017

FOR YEARS, FALSE CLAIMS have bubbled from an especially noxious internet crockpot.

The walks on the moon were faked by NASA. The Sept. 11 attacks and the bombing of an Oklahoma City federal building were inside jobs carried out by the United States government. The slaughter of children at Sandy Hook Elementary School in Connecticut did not actually happen but was staged by gun-control advocates, using child actors.

Most people might want to get as far away as possible from this brew of toxins, carried on a website and radio show run by an ally of President Trump.

But not the president.

As he has before, President Trump dipped a ladle into this pot on Monday, asserting in a speech before military leaders in Florida that the "very, very dishonest press doesn't want to report" on episodes of terrorism. The White House followed up by releasing a list of 78 incidents of "Islamic violence" that the administration claims were played down. In fact, nearly all of them were covered by The New York Times and other news outlets, some with multiple reports from journalists around the world.

The falsehood Mr. Trump uttered in his speech on Monday echoes untrue reports of a cover-up of Islamic terrorism that have been made repeatedly on Infowars, a website that traffics in conspiracy theories like those about Sept. 11 and the mass shooting at the elementary school. The site was founded by Alex Jones, on whose radio show Mr. Trump appeared during the primary campaign. "Your reputation is amazing," Mr. Trump told Mr. Jones, promising to return.

Mr. Jones has boasted that his radio show was the source of Mr. Trump's accusation during the Republican primaries that the father of his opponent, Ted Cruz, had connections to Lee Harvey Oswald, who assassinated President John F. Kennedy in 1963. (Mr. Trump mentioned an article in the National Enquirer in making his unsupported allegation.)

Both Mr. Trump and Mr. Jones falsely claimed that President Barack Obama was not born in the United States, and that thousands of Muslims in the New York area cheered the collapse of the twin towers.

Mr. Trump has not endorsed the Jones view of Sept. 11, Oklahoma City or the killings at the school in Connecticut. But in the official efforts 11 years ago to address the conspiracy theories propagated by Mr. Jones and others known as "9/11 Truthers," it is possible to hear a prophetic tone, strikingly relevant for these times.

For the fifth anniversary of the Sept. 11 attacks in 2006, the State Department and a federal science agency issued reports that insisted the catastrophes were caused by hijackers who used commercial airliners as weapons, and not demolitions or missiles, as imagined by conspiracy theorists. In plain English, the scientific finding meant that what people saw with their own eyes, in real time, is what happened: Planes knocked down the buildings.

To establish that beyond doubt, the science agency, the National Institute of Standards and Technology, published a 10,000-page draft report in 2005 (made final in 2008) on the events that led to the collapse of the towers at the World Trade Center, as well as another tall building that failed later in the day.

Because of persistent claims that the trade center was destroyed by a "controlled demolition" rather than the hijacked airliners, it also published a frequently asked questions document that summarized crucial findings.

Had the agency considered the demolition theory central to many of the conspiracy theories? Indeed it had, and detailed all the trails it had followed, using 7,000 video segments, 7,000 photographs, and 236 pieces of steel from the wreckage, and explained who had conducted the studies — 85 government scientists and 125 experts from the private sector and academia.

"In summary, N.I.S.T. found no corroborating evidence for alternative hypotheses suggesting that the W.T.C. towers were brought down by controlled demolition using explosives," the report stated. The agency did not use the term "conspiracy theorists," but instead referred carefully to "so-called 'alternative theory' groups."

More than a decade later, one of the president's chief advisers, Kellyanne Conway, invoked a notion of "alternative facts" in justifying false statements made by the president's spokesman about the size of the crowd at the inauguration.

A few days later, Ms. Conway referred to the "Bowling Green massacre," an event that she conceded the next day had not occurred. It turned out she had made the same reference to a massacre that did not happen in other interviews. "Honest mistakes abound," she wrote on Twitter.

Abounding and abundant: Alternative theories. Alternative facts. Outright lies. The occasional honest mistake.

JIM DWYER writes the About New York column for The New York Times.

A Conspiracy Theory's Journey From Talk Radio to Trump's Twitter

BY PETER BAKER AND MAGGIE HABERMAN | MARCH 5, 2017

WASHINGTON — It began at 6 p.m. Thursday as a conspiratorial rant on conservative talk radio: President Barack Obama had used the "instrumentalities of the federal government" to wiretap the Republican seeking to succeed him. This "is the big scandal," Mark Levin, the host, told his listeners.

By Friday morning, the unsubstantiated allegation had been picked up by Breitbart News, the site once headed by President Trump's chief strategist, Stephen K. Bannon. Less than 24 hours later, the president embraced the conspiracy in a series of Twitter posts accusing his predecessor of spying on him, setting in motion the latest head-spinning, did-he-really-say-that furor of Mr. Trump's six-week-old presidency.

Previous presidents usually measured their words to avoid a media feeding frenzy, but Mr. Trump showed again over the weekend that he feeds off the frenzy. Uninhibited by the traditional protocols of his office, he makes the most incendiary assertions based on shreds of suspicion. He does so without consulting some of his most senior aides, or even agencies of his own government that might have contrary information. After setting off a public firestorm with no proof, he then calls for an investigation to find the missing evidence.

To his adversaries, Mr. Trump's bomb-throwing seems like a calculated strategy to distract from another story he wants to avoid. In this case, they said Sunday, he clearly wanted to turn the conversation away from Attorney General Jeff Sessions, who recused himself last week from any federal investigation into the Trump campaign's links with Russia in response to reports that he had met with Russia's ambassador during the presidential race. Instead of what Mr. Sessions did or did not do, the Sunday talk shows were dominated by discussion about what Mr. Obama did or did not do.

But in shifting the story, Mr. Trump also kept the Russia investigation front and center, rather than his initiatives on health care, taxes or jobs. His first address to Congress, which won him plaudits for being presidential, was last week but now feels ages ago. Even some Republicans pointed out that if an eavesdropping warrant had been approved, it would mean that a judge was convinced that someone in Mr. Trump's circle might have committed a crime or acted as a foreign agent.

"I'm very worried that our president is suggesting that the former president has done something illegally," Senator Lindsey Graham, Republican of South Carolina, told the audience at a town hall-style meeting in his home state over the weekend. At the same time, he said, "I would be very worried if, in fact, the Obama administration was able to obtain a warrant lawfully about Trump campaign activity with a foreign government."

This was hardly the first time Mr. Trump made a shocking accusation without evidence. He claimed that more than three million people voted against him illegally in November, giving Hillary Clinton a victory in the popular vote. Republican and Democratic officials alike said there was no indication of any such thing, and Mr. Trump's promised investigation has so far led nowhere.

Nor was it the first time Mr. Trump leveled astonishing allegations against Mr. Obama. He spent years promoting the false claim that Mr. Obama was not born in the United States, promising an investigation to uncover the truth and backing down only last year, during his campaign. And last summer, he asserted that Mr. Obama was "the founder of ISIS."

The White House remained firm on Sunday even after Mr. Obama's office denied ordering a wiretap and James R. Clapper Jr., the former director of national intelligence, said on NBC's "Meet the Press" that there had been no wiretapping of Mr. Trump or his campaign. James B. Comey, the F.B.I. director, privately asked the Justice Department to issue a statement that Mr. Trump's claim was false, senior officials said, but the department had not done so as of Sunday evening.

TODD HEISLER/THE NEW YORK TIMES

The lobby of Trump Tower in New York. President Trump alleged, without evidence, that the Obama administration ordered a wiretap of the building.

"Everybody acts like President Trump is the one that came up with this idea and just threw it out there," Sarah Huckabee Sanders, a White House spokeswoman, said on "This Week" on ABC News. "There are multiple news outlets that have reported this. And all we're asking is that we get the same level of look into the Obama administration and the potential that they had for a complete abuse of power that they've been claiming that we have done over the last six months."

Ms. Sanders pointed to reports in "multiple outlets," including The New York Times, as the foundation for the allegation. Mr. Levin, the radio host, likewise read from a series of mainstream news reports during an appearance on "Fox & Friends" on Sunday.

"The evidence is overwhelming," he said. "This is not about President Trump's tweeting. This is about the Obama administration's spying, and the question isn't whether it spied." He added, "The question is who they did spy on, the extent of the spying — that is, the Trump campaign, the Trump transition, Trump surrogates."

But the news organizations he and Ms. Sanders cited have not reported that Mr. Obama tapped Mr. Trump's phones, as the president claimed on Twitter. The Times has reported that several of Mr. Trump's associates are being investigated for their connections with Russians and that law enforcement agencies have examined intercepted communications. It has not reported that those associates themselves have necessarily been wiretapped, but it has reported surveillance of Russians, which is commonplace.

News outlets have noted that a phone call between Michael T. Flynn, Mr. Trump's first national security adviser, and Russia's ambassador to the United States, Sergey I. Kislyak, was monitored, leading to Mr. Flynn's resignation because his account of the conversation did not match the intercept. It is common for the United States to monitor the communications of Russia's ambassador.

The Times also reported that before leaving office, Obama officials tried to spread information about Russian meddling in the election and possible links between Russia and Trump associates, in order to leave a trail for government investigators.

Some Republicans suggested that Mr. Trump might have extrapolated that into an unfounded assertion. "I think the president was not correct, certainly, in saying that President Obama ordered a tap on a server in Trump Tower," former Attorney General Michael B. Mukasey said on "This Week." "However, I think he's right in that there was surveillance and that it was conducted at the behest of the attorney — of the Justice Department," through the special court that authorizes eavesdropping on suspected foreign agents inside the United States.

Conservative radio hosts like Mr. Levin and Rush Limbaugh have focused on Mr. Obama's "tactics" for a while. But it was not until Breitbart published its story that the specific claims crossed Mr. Trump's desk.

Mr. Trump's aides — including Mr. Bannon, an anti-establishment figure who has long questioned the motives of parts of the extensive intelligence bureaucracy — have believed for a long time that the Obama administration colluded with federal investigators who were searching for activity between Russian officials and the Trump campaign surrounding the hacking of Democratic National Committee emails.

They have never offered evidence, but Mr. Trump has long dabbled in conspiracy theories. So when Mr. Trump became aware of the claims in the Breitbart article, aides said, they were appealing to him. It was not immediately clear if someone printed the article out for him or if it was part of a collection of Twitter posts and news articles that his aides present to him each day. But it resonated.

Aides say Mr. Trump went into Friday in a foul mood. He had not known ahead of time that Mr. Sessions planned to recuse himself and never thought he should, even after Mr. Sessions acknowledged that he had talked to Mr. Kislyak despite suggesting otherwise in his Senate confirmation hearing.

Mr. Trump told some advisers that he thought Mr. Sessions had fumbled his answer at that hearing. But on Friday morning in an angry session in the Oval Office, the president railed at aides about the recusal, singling out the White House counsel's office and the communications staff in a tirade visible through the window to a nearby television camera.

Still upset after arriving at Mar-a-Lago, his estate in Palm Beach, Fla., Mr. Trump woke up Saturday morning and began posting on Twitter at 6:26 a.m. In a burst of six messages, he tried to turn the tables by noting that members of the Obama administration also met with Russia's ambassador. Without citing a source, he asserted that Mr. Obama had tapped his phones, and compared it to Watergate. "Bad (or sick) guy," the president wrote.

While the political world erupted over the allegation, Mr. Trump was adamant in conversations throughout the day that he was on to something. His chief strategist, Mr. Bannon, the former Breitbart chairman, flew down to Florida with Donald F. McGahn II, the White House counsel, on Saturday.

Late Saturday morning, Mr. Trump's aides spoke about how to get him to stop posting on Twitter, to avoid opening himself up to further problems. He golfed a little, then returned to the club and began working the phones. At dinner, he roamed the patio, telling a friend, Chris Ruddy, the chief executive of Newsmax Media, that his claims about Mr. Obama would prove true. By Sunday, advisers said, he was fuming that more people were not defending him.

And so he doubled down, calling for a congressional investigation.

"Reports concerning potentially politically motivated investigations immediately ahead of the 2016 election are very troubling," Mr. Trump's press secretary, Sean Spicer, said on Twitter. Until then, he said, the president will not comment further.

PETER BAKER reported from Washington, and **MAGGIE HABERMAN** from New York. **MICHAEL D. SHEAR** contributed reporting from West Palm Beach, Fla.

With 'Spygate,' Trump Shows How He Uses Conspiracy Theories to Erode Trust

ANALYSIS | BY JULIE HIRSCHFELD DAVIS AND MAGGIE HABERMAN | MAY 28, 2018

WASHINGTON — As a candidate, Donald J. Trump claimed that the United States government had known in advance about the Sept. 11 attacks. He hinted that Antonin Scalia, a Supreme Court justice who died in his sleep two years ago, had been murdered. And for years, Mr. Trump pushed the notion that President Barack Obama had been born in Kenya rather than Honolulu, making him ineligible for the presidency.

None of that was true.

Last week, President Trump promoted new, unconfirmed accusations to suit his political narrative: that a "criminal deep state" element within Mr. Obama's government planted a spy deep inside his presidential campaign to help his rival, Hillary Clinton, win — a scheme he branded "Spygate." It was the latest indication that a president who has for decades trafficked in conspiracy theories has brought them from the fringes of public discourse to the Oval Office.

Now that he is president, Mr. Trump's baseless stories of secret plots by powerful interests appear to be having a distinct effect. Among critics, they have fanned fears that he is eroding public trust in institutions, undermining the idea of objective truth and sowing widespread suspicions about the government and news media that mirror his own.

"The effect on the life of the nation of a president inventing conspiracy theories in order to distract attention from legitimate investigations or other things he dislikes is corrosive," said Jon Meacham, a presidential historian and biographer. "The diabolical brilliance of the Trump strategy of disinformation is that many people are simply going to hear the charges and countercharges, and decide that there must be something to them because the president of the United States is saying them."

The effects were evident in Washington on Thursday, when the Justice Department held a pair of unusual briefings with lawmakers to share sensitive information about the special counsel investigation into Russia's meddling in the 2016 election and whether the Trump campaign worked with Moscow to sway the contest. Those sessions came about because the president publicly hectored the department to cough up information about an F.B.I. informant he branded a political spy against him.

But Mr. Trump's willingness to peddle suspicion as fact has implications beyond the Russia inquiry. It is a vital ingredient in the president's communications arsenal, a social media-fueled, brashly expressed narrative of dubious accusations and dark insinuations that allows him to promote his own version of reality.

ERIC THAYER FOR THE NEW YORK TIMES

President Trump's promotion of elaborate, unproven theories appears to be having a distinct effect.

Students of Mr. Trump's life and communication style argue that the idea of conspiracies is a vital part of his strategy to avoid accountability and punch back at detractors, real or perceived, including the news media.

"He's the blame shifter in chief," said Gwenda Blair, a Trump biographer. "Conspiracies, by definition, are things that others do to you. You're being duped; you're being fooled; the world is laughing at us. It goes to this idea that you can't believe anything that you read or see. He has sold us a whole way of accepting a narrative that has so many layers of unaccountable, unsubstantiated content that you can't possibly peel it all back."

Like most conspiracy theories, Mr. Trump's latest has a kernel of truth many Republicans have latched on to. Several news organizations, including The New York Times, have reported that an F.B.I. informant contacted Trump campaign aides who evidence suggested had had suspicious contacts with Russians in 2016 as part of a counterintelligence investigation into possible efforts by Moscow to meddle in the election.

In Mr. Trump's telling, however, the informant was a spy sent by Mr. Obama and a cabal inside his Justice Department and the intelligence community who were bent on stopping his candidacy.

Former aides to the president, speaking privately because they did not want to embarrass him, said paranoia predisposed him to believe in nefarious, hidden forces driving events. But they also said political opportunism informed his promotion of conspiracy theories. For instance, two former aides said Mr. Trump had resisted using the term "deep state" for months, partly because he believed it made him look too much like a crank.

But Mr. Trump saw that it played well in the conservative news media, and so in November, he began using it, the two aides said. The strategy appears to have yielded results. Several polls have shown a dip in public approval of the special counsel investigation over the past several months, as the president has repeatedly attacked it. And a Monmouth Poll released in March found that a bipartisan majority believes an unelected "deep state" is manipulating national policy.

Sam Nunberg, a former Trump aide who worked for him when he began championing false claims about Mr. Obama's birthplace, said the president was reflecting the media that fueled his core supporters.

"In the new media landscape, InfoWars and Fox News are where the president's getting his support, and these theories are promulgated there," said Mr. Nunberg, who disputed that "Spygate" qualified as a conspiracy theory.

Mr. Trump's talk of conspiracies has also gained currency within a Republican Party establishment that once shunned it.

During the 2016 campaign, Senator Lindsey Graham, Republican of South Carolina, denounced Mr. Trump's talk of the government hiding the real story about Sept. 11. "That's something that really only comes from the kook part of America," Mr. Graham said at the time.

Mr. Graham said he had also been highly skeptical when Mr. Trump insisted last year that Mr. Obama had tapped his phones in Trump Tower, a stunning assertion for which he offered no proof.

"I thought, 'Well, that doesn't seem right to me,' " Mr. Graham said last week. But, he noted, it was later revealed that one of Mr. Trump's former campaign associates, Carter Page, had in fact been under surveillance. And on "Spygate," the senator added, "There seems to be something to this one. I want to find out: Did it happen? Is there a good reason?"

Senator John Cornyn, Republican of Texas, distanced himself from the president's sinister language, but not necessarily the questions he had raised about the informant. "I wouldn't describe it the way he described it," Mr. Cornyn said. "Confidential informant? Spy? I guess he can use his own words."

Then, like many lawmakers who once denounced the president's assaults on law enforcement agencies, Mr. Cornyn gave the president a level of validation, saying it was worth knowing what the F.B.I.'s "motivation" was in the inquiry into the Trump campaign.

Mr. Trump is not the first public figure to charge that he is the subject of a shadowy plot. Mrs. Clinton memorably declared during impeachment proceedings against her husband, Bill Clinton, that they were the victims of a "vast, right-wing conspiracy," although the president himself never used the word at the time.

Mr. Meacham pointed to an 1866 speech at a tumultuous moment of post-Civil War Reconstruction, in which President Andrew Johnson said that his political enemies were plotting to assassinate him. President Richard M. Nixon believed that an elitist cabal led by Ivy League-educated denizens of Georgetown and Washington Post journalists was working secretly to bring him down. Both presidents, Mr. Meacham noted, were self-made men who harbored deep insecurities, not unlike the current Oval Office occupant.

Erick Erickson, the founder of the conservative website RedState, who once described Mr. Trump as a "walking, talking National Enquirer," said the president's invented stories also speak to the public's desire to have an easy explanation for events it cannot control.

"A lot of people really want to believe a conspiracy because it's a lot easier to think a malevolent force is in charge than that our government is run by idiots," Mr. Erickson said in an interview.

Representative Peter T. King, a New York Republican who is sometimes a critic of Mr. Trump, said one need not believe in conspiracies to recognize that the president was onto something with his seemingly far-fetched charges.

"I do believe that people like Clapper, to some extent Comey, they had this bias against him," Mr. King said, naming James R. Clapper Jr., the former director of national intelligence, and James B. Comey, the former F.B.I. director, both viewed by Mr. Trump as enemies bent on his destruction. "I don't think it's a grand conspiracy. I just think they were living in an echo chamber and believed the worst."

But even as he took issue with the president's framing, Mr. King marveled at how the president has bent the discourse to his own views, transforming the term "deep state" into "almost a metaphor for a group in society that doesn't understand real people, forgotten people, and are willing to use their power to stop Trump."

"He has a talent for getting a point across using hyperbole," Mr. King said, adding, "There's no doubt he has changed the debate."

Trump Attacks Sessions and F.B.I., Citing Conspiracy Theories

BY MICHAEL D. SHEAR AND EILEEN SULLIVAN | SEPT. 19, 2018

WASHINGTON — President Trump excoriated on Wednesday his attorney general, the F.B.I., the special counsel and members of the intelligence community — citing conspiracy theories by conservatives even as he declared in a wide-ranging interview that he is "not a conspiratorial person."

Mr. Trump used the Oval Office interview with The Hill newspaper to unleash some of his most deeply felt grievances against his critics, saying that one of the "crowning achievements" of his presidency will be exposing what he calls corruption among the people investigating his administration.

"We have tremendous support, by the way, to expose something that is truly a cancer in our country," the president said of federal law enforcement officials without citing evidence. The remark was a striking rhetorical echo of 1973, when John Dean, the White House counsel, gravely told President Richard M. Nixon that the Watergate scandal was "a cancer within — close to the presidency."

By contrast, Mr. Trump compared his repeated trashing of F.B.I. investigators to congressional passage of tax cuts and the elimination of regulations by his administration, saying that "what we've done is a great service to the country, really."

The president's antipathy toward the intelligence community and the Justice Department has been clear for most of his time in the White House. But Mr. Trump's verbal assault on his own law enforcement agencies during Tuesday's interview was remarkable even by his standards.

Mr. Trump made false assertions about the origins of the Russia investigation and the political makeup of its investigators, citing stories from Fox News personalities: "the great Lou Dobbs, the great Sean Hannity, the wonderful, great Jeanine Pirro."

The president escalated his drawn-out war with Attorney General Jeff Sessions over Mr. Trump's assertion that Mr. Sessions had failed to protect him from the federal investigation into Russia's interference in the 2016 presidential election and whether any Trump associates conspired with it.

"I don't have an attorney general," Mr. Trump declared — an extraordinary statement even for a president who has already called his attorney general weak and disloyal. "It's very sad," he continued.

(On Wednesday morning, Mr. Trump all but reversed himself. "We have an attorney general," he said, in response to reporters' questions as he departed the White House to visit storm-struck North Carolina. "I'm disappointed in the attorney general for many reasons.")

Mr. Trump also continued his barrage against Robert S. Mueller III, the special counsel in the Russia investigation. He said Mr. Mueller was conducting a "fraudulent" inquiry and was "totally conflicted" because of what the president called a "nasty business transaction" between himself and Mr. Mueller years ago.

Mr. Trump did not say what the transaction was, though he has alleged a dispute over membership fees when Mr. Mueller left one of Mr. Trump's golf clubs while he was F.B.I. director.

And he indicated that he asked this week for the declassification of court documents, F.B.I. records and text messages in the Russia inquiry at the urging of members of Congress and "commentators that I respect" on cable news broadcasts.

"I have had many people ask me to release them. Not that I didn't like the idea, but I wanted to wait. I wanted to see what, you know, where it was all going," Mr. Trump said.

Law enforcement and intelligence officials must still vet the declassified materials and redact sensitive information. Declassified court documents and materials released to the public under the Freedom of Information Act often have redactions.

The review of this latest declassification order is being given top priority because the request came from Mr. Trump, officials said. It is still underway and is primarily concerned with protecting sources and methods, a key concern of senior intelligence leaders, according to two officials briefed on the matter.

Should Mr. Trump reject the recommendations of the intelligence community, it could put Justice Department and F.B.I. officials into the uncomfortable position of having to oppose an action taken by the president or to reveal information that they believe undermines national security.

The president reserved some of his harshest words for Mr. Sessions. Asked by reporters on Wednesday whether he planned to fire the attorney general, the president said, "We are looking at lots of different things."

Through an extended barrage of humiliating statements and jabs, Mr. Trump has made clear that Mr. Sessions's job is in peril. At one point, Mr. Sessions, one of the president's earliest prominent supporters, drafted a resignation letter.

The president recently told Bloomberg News that he would not fire Mr. Sessions before the midterm elections in November. And should Mr. Trump decide to dismiss him, it is unlikely that the Senate could confirm a replacement before then.

Mr. Trump has long publicly shamed the attorney general for recusing himself in March 2017 from overseeing the Russia investigation — a sprawling inquiry that has cast a shadow over Mr. Trump's 20 months in office and resulted in convictions and guilty pleas from his former aides.

Mr. Trump already has personal lawyers — nearly a dozen — looking out for his personal and business interests in two federal investigations in Washington and New York. But firing Mr. Sessions would be a way to change who has oversight of the investigation.

In his interview with The Hill, Mr. Trump said his disappointment in Mr. Sessions extended to immigration, an issue on which both men share a hard-line view.

"I'm not happy at the border," Mr. Trump said. "I'm not happy with numerous things."

The Justice Department declined to comment.

In the interview with The Hill, Mr. Trump also said he regretted not firing his first F.B.I. director, James B. Comey, earlier. Appointed by President Barack Obama, Mr. Comey was less than four years into a 10-year term when Mr. Trump abruptly fired him in May 2017.

"If I did one mistake with Comey, I should have fired him before I got here. I should have fired him the day I won the primaries," Mr. Trump said. "I should have fired him right after the convention. Say, 'I don't want that guy.' Or at least fired him the first day on the job."

The special counsel's office is examining the firing of Mr. Comey as part of its inquiry into whether Mr. Trump tried to obstruct the investigation by removing the F.B.I. director.

JULIAN E. BARNES, **KATIE BENNER** and **EMILY COCHRANE** contributed reporting.

Did Democrats, or George Soros, Fund Migrant Caravan? Despite Republican Claims, No

BY LINDA QIU | OCT. 20, 2018

WHAT WAS SAID

"BUT A LOT OF MONEY *has been passing to people to come up and try and get to the border by Election Day, because they think that's a negative for us. ... They have lousy policy. The one thing, they stick together, but they wanted that caravan and there are those that say that caravan didn't just happen. It didn't just happen. A lot of reasons that caravan, 4,000 people."*

— President Trump, at a campaign rally in Missoula, Mont., on Thursday

THE FACTS

This lacks evidence.

A caravan of migrants is traveling north toward Mexico and the United States — and prompting alarm and false claims from Mr. Trump and Representative Matt Gaetz, Republican of Florida.

There is no evidence that George Soros, a billionaire and major Democratic donor, paid thousands of migrants to "storm." Nor is there evidence that Democrats support the effort, as Mr. Trump has said.

Mr. Gaetz is wrong about several things in his description of the video he posted.

First, it was not shot in Honduras, which he later acknowledged. Google Maps and Facebook photos place the storefront seen in the video, an auto parts shop, in Chiquimula, Guatemala. As Kirk Semple of The New York Times reported, the migrant caravan was formed last week in San Pedro Sula, Honduras, and has made its way north through Guatemala.

Second, Mr. Gaetz's speculation that the migrants were being offered cash to join the caravan by Mr. Soros is unfounded. Open

Society Foundations, Mr. Soros's philanthropic organization, has denied any involvement.

Luis Assardo, a Guatemalan journalist, said in an email that he spoke to residents of Chiquimula and was told that some local merchants had given the migrants money while others had offered food, clothing or other help.

The video appears to show each migrant receiving a single bill, so the largest amount they could have received was 200 quetzales, equal to about $26. Migrants in the caravan told The New York Times that the Guatemalans generally handed out one or two quetzals, or about 13 to 26 cents — undercutting Mr. Trump's claim of "a lot of money" exchanging hands.

The migrants said they were not paid to join the caravan.

In an interview, Mr. Gaetz says he now suspects that the men handing out money were cartel members sowing good will and seeking to subvert the government. He is also concerned that American nongovernmental organizations were involved in organizing the caravan, but concedes that "they may not be." He emphasized that he was merely asking questions — and is "still asking."

The notion that refugees will leave their homes solely for a little cash is "crazy," said Alex Mensing, a project coordinator with Pueblo Sin Fronteras, a transnational group that organized the migrant caravan that captured Mr. Trump's attention last spring. (The group did not coordinate the caravan that is now traveling north, but has been organizing similar journeys for years.)

"You don't have to pay people to try to save their own lives," Mr. Mensing said. "They are fleeing violence, death threats or economic violence."

There is similarly no evidence that Democrats "wanted that caravan." Though Democrats (and many Republicans) oppose the Trump administration's policy of separating families detained at the border, Democrats have supported legislation to improve border security.

Daniel Wessel, a spokesman for the Democratic National Committee, pointed to legislation proposed in the Senate that tries to "address the root causes of the Central American migrant crisis" by expanding refugee processing in other countries and targeting drug cartels.

"Trump has turned to fear-mongering and conspiracy theories in order to push his anti-immigrant agenda," Mr. Wessel said.

MAYA AVERBUCH contributed reporting from Guatemala, and **MEGAN SPECIA** from New York.

LINDA QIU is a fact-check reporter, based in Washington. She came to The Times in 2017 from the fact-checking service PolitiFact.

How Trump-Fed Conspiracy Theories About Migrant Caravan Intersect With Deadly Hatred

ANALYSIS | BY JEREMY W. PETERS | OCT. 29, 2018

MURPHYSBORO, ILL. — Alicia Hooten thinks the country has plenty of problems. "So many; so many," she said warily, before settling on the one at the top of her mind with the midterm election just a week away. "I feel like we're fighting for our freedom when it comes to our borders."

She spoke while waiting for President Trump's campaign rally on Saturday, hours after the deadly shootings in Pittsburgh. Ms. Hooten, a graphic designer from nearby Sparta, Ill., said she was especially concerned about the caravan of migrants in southern Mexico, calling it "a ploy to destroy America, and to bring us to our knees."

"I'm not going to take it — not going to go down without a fight," she insisted.

For the last two weeks, Mr. Trump and his conservative allies have operated largely in tandem on social media and elsewhere to push alarmist, conspiratorial warnings about the migrant caravan more than 2,000 miles from the border. They have largely succeeded in animating Republican voters like Ms. Hooten around the idea of these foreign nationals posing a dire threat to the country's security, stability and identity.

Mr. Trump described them as "an invasion of our country" on Monday, and his administration announced plans to deploy at least 5,200 active-duty troops to the southern border by the end of this week, its biggest show of force yet in confronting the migrants.

But as the country processes the cumulative trauma of two actual crises that occurred inside its borders — a spate of pipe bombs sent to the president's political opponents, and the massacre of 11 people at a synagogue by a man who spewed anti-Semitic vitriol and called immigrants "invaders" — there is clear overlap between the hatred and delusion that drove this lethal behavior and the paranoia and misinformation surrounding the caravan.

The baseless claims that George Soros is financing the migrants as they trek north, which carry a strong whiff of anti-Semitism, have been one of the most consistent themes of commentary on the caravan from the right. And their persuasive power was evident over the weekend in interviews at the president's rally in Murphysboro, where several people described Mr. Soros, the liberal billionaire philanthropist, as the caravan's mastermind and made assertions like "I'm positive he's the one behind it," "It looks a tad staged," and "All these people are being paid off."

Mr. Trump tweeted a video on Oct. 18 that purported to be of someone connected to Mr. Soros handing out cash to the migrants — one of several insinuations and attacks on Mr. Soros by Republican leaders and candidates this fall. Then, on Oct. 22, a pipe bomb was found at Mr. Soros's house; the police have charged a Trump supporter, Cesar Sayoc, with mailing the bombs to Mr. Soros and other Democrats whom the president frequently criticizes.

Robert Bowers, who was arrested in the assault on the Pittsburgh synagogue, also pushed online conspiracy theories about the migrant caravan, in addition to anti-Semitic diatribes.

Mr. Trump and Republican officials have shown no signs of backing off their approach to stoking fears about the caravan in the final days of the election season. Just a few hours after the synagogue killings on Saturday, Mr. Trump again referred to the midterms as "the election of the caravan," as he has done at other political rallies recently.

"The reason why the caravan has resonated so much on the right is because it is the literal, physical representation of what Republicans don't want to see happening at the border," said Andy Surabian, a former aide to the Trump presidential campaign and White House. "I can't imagine a clearer picture to be painted to illustrate this issue to Trump voters."

TOM BRENNER FOR THE NEW YORK TIMES

President Trump, who attended a rally in Wisconsin last week before this audience, is trying to draw the attention of Republican voters back to issues like immigration, which have always sparked enthusiasm among the Republican grassroots.

With the kind of dark language usually reserved for true catastrophes like the Sept. 11 attacks, conservative commentators and politicians have led a concerted push to elevate the caravan as an issue. They have called it "an invasion," "a national emergency," "an illegal alien mob," "an attack on America" and a crisis with implications that are "critical to the future of our civilization."

These outcries, which have included unfounded claims about the caravan's origins and wildly fluctuating estimates of its size, are playing out in a clear pattern. They often start with right-wing commentators, conspiracy theorists and activist groups with large followings; their talk then breaks through more broadly on Fox News, Breitbart News and other outlets that are popular with conservative voters; and ultimately Mr. Trump tweets or remarks about them, acting as an amplifier and a validator.

Apart from concerns of domestic terrorism, any number of threats, foreign and domestic, have been simmering in the weeks leading to the election, like the killing of a Washington Post columnist inside the Saudi Consulate in Istanbul, though none of them have received as much attention from the president and his allies as the migrant caravan.

Even a massacre of fellow Americans lacks the singular power of illegal immigration as a galvanizing factor for some fervent Trump supporters. And no immigration issue is as vividly captured as the caravan — in images and videos broadcast repeatedly and shared widely on social media, some of them misleading or unproven, that show thousands of Latin Americans making their way toward the United States. The president has shared some of these mislabeled images himself.

That imagery has also made the caravan ripe for exploitation by conservatives who have spoken in hyperbolic, sometimes frightening terms. Over the weekend, Breitbart News posted a story about the migrants possibly having "diseases that could pose a threat to public health."

"Fox & Friends," the president's preferred morning news program, aired an interview on Sunday with a man who said through an interpreter that he was trying to get to the United States so he could ask for a pardon for his attempted-murder conviction.

Newt Gingrich, the former House speaker and a confidante of Mr. Trump's, surmised in an interview with Fox News, "If you were a terrorist and wanted to get in the United States and you saw 10,000 people trying to get into the United States, how unlikely is it that you might decide to join them?"

(The size of the caravan has fluctuated over the course of the last two weeks, but it now numbers in the thousands.)

Michael Savage, the conservative radio host, estimated the caravan's size at 14,000 on his program last week as he predicted that its eventual arrival would spell "the end of America as we know it."

Mr. Trump believes that focusing on illegal immigration is a winning strategy for him, and his advisers have come to share that view, armed with polling data that show that the issue continues to be a top priority for Republican base voters. They are using the caravan to raise broader fears as well about what they portray as a broken, permissive immigration system that is weakening the country culturally, financially and even physically.

Republican officials are aware of the political downside of highlighting the issue, which tends to turn off suburban women and college-educated white voters, but they have calculated that using fear of crime and terrorism can neutralize that disadvantage. And they believe that Democrats have overplayed their hands on immigration because of calls by some of their prominent leaders for the abolition of Immigration and Customs Enforcement, the agency responsible for deportations.

That is why Mr. Trump — and many Republican candidates who have followed his lead — have been touting their support for ICE and highlighting MS-13, the brutal transnational gang with roots in El Salvador, as well as the risks of so-called sanctuary cities that limit their cooperation with the federal immigration authorities.

Of the dozen people interviewed at Mr. Trump's rally, almost all of them spoke in considerable detail about their concerns over immigration. Ms. Hooten, the Trump supporter at the rally on Saturday, blamed Mr. Soros, Hillary Clinton and former President Barack Obama for the caravan.

"I think they're all involved in this," she said. "I feel it's treason."

Another person at the rally, Jeff Hutson of Columbus, Ky., called the caravan "a smoke screen" — no different from a lot of other big news stories he said he thinks are intended to distract Americans. "I think we've had a lot of that going on," he said. "I think a lot of the shootings we've had — anything big to draw attention away from something else that's going on."

The language and imagery of danger lurking within the caravan started almost immediately after its existence was reported this month. In some cases, as evident from the unproven claim that Middle Easterners were hiding among the migrants, that rhetoric traces a path from right-wing activists online to Mr. Trump.

The Center for Immigration Studies, a group the president has cited in the past for its research promoting his immigration policies, was among the first to report on Oct. 16 on claims by the president of Guatemala — made before the caravan had formed — that his country had captured and deported 100 people with ties to ISIS.

On Oct. 18, Judicial Watch, a conservative group that spends much of its time on endeavors like lawsuits to retrieve documents from Hillary Clinton's time as secretary of state and investigations of alleged voter fraud, published a piece on the Guatemalan president's statement, warning: "Why should Americans care about this? A caravan of Central American migrants is making its way north."

Three days later, on Oct. 21, the group's president, Tom Fitton, appeared on "Fox & Friends" to discuss its report and said that Guatemala had become "a way station" for terrorists.

The next morning, at 8:37, Mr. Trump tweeted about the caravan, "Criminals and unknown Middle Easterners are mixed in," a claim he later walked back because he said he did not have evidence. The next day, however, a Department of Homeland Security official tweeted that citizens from all over the world, including the Middle East, were traveling with the caravan.

Not that such alarming language is out of the ordinary for the president. At a political rally in Kentucky this month, Mr. Trump declared that Democrats "want to open America's borders and turn our country into a friendly sanctuary for murderous thugs from other countries who will kill us all."

JULIE HIRSCHFELD DAVIS and **MICHAEL D. SHEAR** contributed reporting.

CHAPTER 5

Alex Jones, False Flags and Crisis Actors

Among the most prominent voices of conspiracy is Alex Jones, host of the popular radio show The Alex Jones Show and owner of the website Infowars.com. Jones has become known for suggesting that survivors and family members of mass shootings are "crisis actors," or individuals paid to depict a tragedy, as part of a leftist conspiracy. The articles in this chapter chart his influence and examine how he has forced the media to respond to his vocal support of conspiracy.

After Orlando Shooting, 'False Flag' and 'Crisis Actor' Conspiracy Theories Surface

BY CHRISTOPHER MELE | JUNE 28, 2016

AFTER THE MASS SHOOTING at a gay nightclub in Orlando, Fla., on June 12, Twitter brimmed with news reports of the carnage. But some posts on the massacre that claimed 49 lives also included a curious phrase: "false flag."

It was a code used by conspiracy theorists to signal their belief that the government had staged the massacre and the information the public was reading and hearing from the mainstream media was untrue.

The victims in the shooting? They were "crisis actors" hired to promote the story as a pretext to impose tighter gun restrictions, the theory goes.

I believe that there is no such "massacre" and that it is a #falseflag operation for political purposes. #Orlando https://t.co/BvONlsSMrb

— LaLegale (@LaLegale) June 13, 2016

It is easy to dismiss such beliefs as preposterous and to think of them as coming from a paranoid fringe of society that deeply distrusts the government, but such theories are pervasive. It is difficult to gauge how many people believe these stories, but a general search of YouTube for false-flag videos brought up more than 700,000 results.

The term false flag relates to naval warfare when a ship would fly a flag that would conceal its true identity as a way to lure an enemy closer. Today, it is commonly a shorthand for an act of deception.

Conspiracy theorists have applied the label to high-profile attacks, including the shootings by a husband and wife last year in San Bernardino, Calif., that killed 14; the massacre at Sandy Hook Elementary School in Newtown, Conn., in 2012 that left 26 dead; and the attack at Virginia Tech in Blacksburg, Va., in 2007 that killed 33.

The phrase has even been used to doubt the Sept. 11 terrorist attacks.

Jesse Walker, the author of "The United States of Paranoia: A Conspiracy Theory," said fear, the human need to find patterns and tell stories, and the recognition that conspiracies are not impossible help fuel such theories. The stories — no matter how outlandish — can bring meaning and a measure of comfort in a world that can make no sense, he said.

False-flag theories have long been around. One focused on the assassination attempt in 1835 of President Andrew Jackson, during which the president fought off a gunman whose two weapons misfired.

Conspiracy theorists at the time believed Jackson had hired the gunman as a way to drum up sympathy for himself, Mr. Walker said.

Unlike the 1800s, stories today benefit from instant delivery through the internet and social media. One of the better-known purveyors is Alex Jones, who hosts an internet show at the website infowars.com. The day of the Orlando shooting, he posted a video in which he asserted that the government had let the massacre happen so it could pass "hate laws to deal with right-wingers" and to disarm gun owners. He did not respond to an email seeking comment.

Mike Rothschild of Pasadena, Calif., who has researched and written about conspiracy theories, described the world of false-flag believers as a "bank of awakened internet sleuths that has got it all figured out." They see it as their duty to warn others about secret elites in government who are plotting against citizens, he said.

If overwhelming concrete evidence debunks the theorists' notions, it only reinforces their ideas, said Chip Berlet, a researcher of radical-right movements and retired analyst at Political Research Associates, a left-leaning think tank in Somerville, Mass. For conspiracy believers, explaining it away "shows how smart the enemy really is," he said.

Rob Brotherton, a psychologist and science journalist who wrote "Suspicious Minds: Why We Believe Conspiracy Theories," said it is not just false-flaggers who seek connections and hidden meanings in world events.

"Everybody loves a story with a good plot twist, which is basically what conspiracy theories are," he wrote in an email. "Conspiracy theories arguably just have slightly different logic and standards of evidence."

But does paying attention to such theories give them legitimacy? Mr. Rothschild said it was better for the public to be knowledgeable about rather than blindsided by such stories.

Another conspiracy researcher, Joseph E. Uscinski, a political science professor at the University of Miami, has noted that such theories rarely go unchallenged and are frequently debunked on the internet, Mr. Brotherton said.

Still, trying to quash conspiracists can be a no-win proposition.

"For someone who believes in a conspiracy, you can't go wrong," Derek Arnold, who teaches communications at Villanova University in Pennsylvania, wrote in an email.

"If the powers that be give you information that is against your theory, it's a lie; if it supports your theory, you are even more vindicated. And if they stay silent, it's because you've got something to hide."

He Calls Hillary Clinton a 'Demon.' Who Is Alex Jones?

BY LIAM STACK | OCT. 13, 2016

PRESIDENT OBAMA took a moment at a rally this week to sniff his hand to prove that he is not really a demon from hell who reeks of sulfur and walks the Earth swarmed by flies. Why would the president of the United States do such a thing, even in jest?

"I was reading the other day there is a guy on the radio who apparently — Trump's on his show frequently — he said me and Hillary are demons," Mr. Obama explained to the laughing crowd. "Said we smelled like sulfur. Ain't that something?"

He then lifted his hand, took a sniff, and broke into a broad grin. "Now, I mean, come on people!"

The radio host in question was Alex Jones, who on Monday called Hillary Clinton "an abject psychopathic demon from hell" who was bent on destroying the planet.

"She's so dark now and so evil and so possessed" that her very presence inflicts nightmares upon those in close physical proximity to her, he said.

"I been told this by high up folks and they tell me Obama and Hillary both smell like sulfur," he said in his trademark style, a kind of shout that mixes bombast and panic. "They smell like hell."

Mr. Obama may laugh off Mr. Jones fire-and-brimstone rantings, but many people do not. He is an influential, if fringe, conservative figure whose radio show, videos and websites peddle conspiracy theories to an audience of millions.

Here is a brief introduction.

WHERE DOES HE WORK?

Mr. Jones is based in Texas, where he hosts The Alex Jones Show, a nationally syndicated talk show, and runs Infowars, a website he founded that offers an angry and histrionic take on the day's news. He has been called "the most prolific conspiracy theorist in contemporary America" by the Southern Poverty Law Center, which tracks hate groups.

The Alex Jones Show says it is broadcast on 160 radio stations, but his influence is perhaps most keenly felt on the internet. More than 1.6 million people have subscribed to his YouTube channel, where video clips from his show have been watched almost one billion times since 2008. Another 1.2 million people have liked his Facebook page and over 470,000 follow him on Twitter.

Mr. Jones has had several bursts of mainstream attention. In 2011 he aired an interview with Charlie Sheen that led to the actor's dismissal from the sitcom "Two and a Half Men." Two years later he started an online petition to deport the CNN host Piers Morgan, a British citizen, from the United States because of his advocacy of gun control laws.

Mr. Morgan invited Mr. Jones onto his show to debate gun control, but it quickly devolved into more than 10 minutes of red-faced screaming by Mr. Jones, who affected a British accent and called Mr. Morgan "a hatchet man of the New World Order."

"I am here to tell you, 1776 will commence again if you try to take our firearms," he yelled. "Doesn't matter how many lemmings you get out there on the street begging for them to have their guns taken, we will not relinquish them. Do you understand?"

WHAT DOES HE BELIEVE?

Mr. Jones has described himself as a libertarian. Many of his views mix traditional conservative critiques of government with wild-eyed delusions about globe-spanning conspiracies. His main focus is a supposed liberal plot to seize people's guns and install a tyrannical world government.

There is almost no major news event that Mr. Jones has not woven into that conspiracy narrative. He argues that the Sept. 11, 2001, terrorist attacks and the Oklahoma City bombing were "inside jobs" committed by rogue elements of the "military industrial complex." He says the Sandy Hook shooting was a hoax perpetrated by forces hostile to the Second Amendment. The list goes on.

Mr. Jones argued in 2013 that same-sex marriage was a "eugenicist globalist" plot "to encourage the breakdown of the family" and "get rid of God" so the state can reign supreme. "Not because they're atheists, but because they want the state to be God," he said.

HOW DOES HE FIT INTO THE PRESIDENTIAL RACE?

Mr. Jones is a fervent supporter of Donald J. Trump, who appeared on The Alex Jones Show for a 30-minute interview in December 2015. "What you are doing is epic, it's George Washington level," Mr. Jones told Mr. Trump.

Mr. Jones enthusiastically endorsed Mr. Trump's positions on immigration and terrorism and at the end of the interview the Republican candidate praised the host for his integrity. "Your reputation is amazing," Mr. Trump said. "I will not let you down. You will be very, very impressed, I hope. And I think we'll be speaking a lot."

HAS HILLARY CLINTON ADDRESSED HIS CLAIMS?

Yes, she has.

Mrs. Clinton condemned Mr. Jones during a speech in August that criticized Mr. Trump for his support among the "alt-right," a radical group of conspiracy theorists and white nationalists on the fringe of the conservative movement.

She compared his radio show to The National Enquirer and called his claims that the Sandy Hook shooting was a hoax "disgusting."

"I don't know what happens in somebody's mind or how dark their heart must be to say things like that, but Trump doesn't challenge these lies," Mrs. Clinton said.

For Mr. Jones, though, all publicity seems to be good publicity.

Hours after Mrs. Clinton spoke, his show ran a long segment on her criticisms. He denied much of what she said but basked in her attention, using her remarks as an opportunity to portray himself as a noble warrior for the truth.

"She attacked the resistance to her takeover of this country by foreign banks, the Saudi Arabian government, the Communist Chinese and others," he said. "She's in deep trouble."

Las Vegas Massacre Gives InfoWars More Conspiracy Fodder

BY MICHAEL M. GRYNBAUM | OCT. 9, 2017

THE MYSTERY OF WHY Stephen Paddock smuggled an arsenal into a Las Vegas hotel room before firing into a crowd of concertgoers, killing dozens and injuring hundreds, has only deepened in the days since the massacre. His motives remain elusive, his beliefs unclear.

That absence of information has provided an opening for right-wing media personalities like Alex Jones of InfoWars to proffer their own theories. Their ideas, often based on scant evidence, fall in line with common right-wing tropes about liberal conspiracies, and millions of Americans are listening.

Mr. Jones — who has propagated conspiracy theories about the Sandy Hook Elementary School massacre in 2012 and the Sept. 11, 2001, terror attacks — has portrayed Mr. Paddock by turns as an agent of the Islamic State, a leftist activist, an anti-Trump radical and a possible stooge for a broader conspiracy intent on disrupting democracy.

"Could Stephen Paddock, the lone Vegas shooter, have been a patsy to kick off the left's war with the right in the streets of America?" Mr. Jones wrote on his Facebook page last week. The post accompanied a video titled "Video Shows Second Shooter During Vegas Massacre," which by Monday had been viewed about 1.1 million times.

Investigators have worked feverishly to identify a motivation behind Mr. Paddock's attack. Followers of InfoWars, however, heard a black-and-white story in the days after the mass shooting.

"Clearly, there's more than one shooter," Mr. Jones said on his Friday radio show, citing high-ranking law enforcement officials whom he declined to name. "They said there's no way he acted alone," Mr. Jones added. "He had help."

InfoWars has backed its claim of an accomplice by highlighting supposed evidence like a room service receipt from Mr. Paddock's hotel room, which seemed to suggest two guests were present. So far, the authorities have said Mr. Paddock was the sole gunman.

Still, the fluid nature of the investigation has generated reports by mainstream outlets that can offer fuel for the conspiracy-minded. NBC News, for instance, reported on Friday afternoon that investigators had found a smartphone charger in Mr. Paddock's hotel room that did not match his phones. Later, NBC News updated its report, saying the charger had been accounted for, and quoted a Las Vegas police official who was "confident" that nobody else had been in the room.

By Sunday, Mr. Jones had not backed down. "It's a fact InfoWars has been the most accurate media operation so far, telling you that he did not act alone," he said in a video posted to his Facebook page.

Mr. Jones's spin on Mr. Paddock has been amplified thanks to The Drudge Report. The influential website splashed several InfoWars stories about the massacre across its traffic-driving home page last week, whooshing Mr. Jones's theories onto millions of screens.

HILARY SWIFT FOR THE NEW YORK TIMES

Mr. Jones at a rally in Cleveland during the Republican National Convention last year. "Clearly, there's more than one shooter," he said on his radio show on Friday.

In Sunday's video, Mr. Jones acknowledged the help. "Thanks to DrudgeReport.com magnifying those articles, having the courage to run our articles, a lot of people are now able to get more information to the police, and more information to the media," he said.

This is not the first time InfoWars has spread unfounded theories about national tragedies. Mr. Jones repeated false rumors about a child abuse ring at a Washington pizzeria; a North Carolina man later fired a gun inside the restaurant. (Mr. Jones later apologized.)

After the gun massacre at Sandy Hook Elementary School in Newtown, Conn., Mr. Jones repeatedly asserted that the episode was "completely fake," prompting some listeners to harass grieving parents of victims. He has also called the 9/11 attacks a hoax and an "inside job."

Mr. Jones's website reached more than 1.4 million unique visitors in June, according to the web tracking firm comScore. (Its numbers fell off in August, to 689,000 visitors; last November, nearly four million people visited.)

Whether Mr. Jones's behavior is merely an act has come under debate: During a custody battle in April, a lawyer for Mr. Jones, Randall Wilhite, said his client was only playing a character. "He's a performance artist," Mr. Wilhite added.

Mr. Jones has insisted in interviews that he is trying to inform an audience that no longer trusts the traditional press. And he has attracted the approval of President Trump, who granted Mr. Jones an interview during the presidential campaign and has retweeted one of the site's personalities, Paul Joseph Watson.

On Wednesday, Roger Stone, an InfoWars contributor and sometime Trump confidant, appeared on air with Mr. Jones to argue that the traditional news media was hiding facts about the Las Vegas massacre from the public.

Before bringing on Mr. Stone as his guest, Mr. Jones said, "All I know is, they're trying to blame gun owners when it was patriots that got targeted. They're making their move. The Democrats have said they're going to have a huge uprising in October, November. It's here."

Citing a "high-level" C.I.A. official and "top psychiatrists from the federal government," Mr. Jones added: "They're saying clearly he's antifa. Clearly, it's the M.O., to trigger a helter-skelter revolution."

Mr. Trump spent several days last week accusing NBC News of fabricating a story about Secretary of State Rex W. Tillerson's referring to the president as a "moron." Asked about the NBC report, Mr. Trump's press secretary, Sarah Huckabee Sanders, said during a White House press briefing that the administration was concerned about falsehoods spreading in the news media.

"We see a problem with any stories that are inaccurate or untruthful being presented to the American people as facts," Ms. Sanders said.

Right-Wing Media Uses Parkland Shooting as Conspiracy Fodder

BY MICHAEL M. GRYNBAUM | FEB. 20, 2018

THE TEENAGERS OF Marjory Stoneman Douglas High School in Parkland, Fla., who a week ago lost 17 of their classmates and school staff members in a mass shooting, have emerged as passionate advocates for reform, speaking openly of their anger in the hope of forcing a reckoning on guns.

But in certain right-wing corners of the web — and, increasingly, from more mainstream voices like Rush Limbaugh and a commentator on CNN — the students are being portrayed not as grief-ridden survivors but as pawns and conspiracists intent on exploiting a tragedy to undermine the nation's laws.

In these baseless accounts, which by Tuesday had spread rapidly on social media, the students are described as "crisis actors," who travel to the sites of shootings to instigate fury against guns. Or they are called F.B.I. plants, defending the bureau for its failure to catch the shooter. They have been portrayed as puppets being coached and manipulated by the Democratic Party, gun control activists, the so-called antifa movement and the left-wing billionaire George Soros.

The theories are far-fetched. But they are finding a broad and prominent audience online. On Tuesday, the president's son Donald J. Trump Jr. liked a pair of tweets that accused David Hogg, a 17-year-old who is among the most outspoken of the Parkland students, of criticizing the Trump administration in an effort to protect his father, whom Mr. Hogg has described as a retired F.B.I. agent.

Mr. Hogg, the high school's student news director, has become a sensation among many liberals for his polished and compelling television interviews, in which he has called on lawmakers to enact tougher restrictions on guns. Just as quickly, Mr. Hogg attracted the disdain of right-wing provocateurs like The Gateway Pundit, a fringe website that gained prominence in 2016 for pushing conspiracies about voter fraud and Hillary Clinton.

In written posts and YouTube videos — one of which had more than 100,000 views as of Tuesday night — Gateway Pundit has argued that Mr. Hogg had been coached on what to say during his interviews. The notion that Mr. Hogg is merely protecting his father dovetails with a broader right-wing trope, that liberal forces in the F.B.I. are trying to undermine President Trump and his pro-Second Amendment supporters.

Others offered more sweeping condemnations. Alex Jones, the conspiracy theorist behind the site Infowars, suggested that the mass shooting was a "false flag" orchestrated by anti-gun groups. Mr. Limbaugh, on his radio program, said of the student activists on Monday: "Everything they're doing is right out of the Democrat Party's various playbooks. It has the same enemies: the N.R.A. and guns."

By Tuesday, that argument had migrated to CNN. In an on-air appearance, Jack Kingston, a former United States representative from Georgia and a regular CNN commentator, asked, "Do we really think — and I say this sincerely — do we really think 17-year-olds on their own are going to plan a nationwide rally?" (He was quickly rebuked by the anchor Alyson Camerota.)

Conspiracies, wild and raw online, are often pasteurized on their way into the mainstream. A subtler version of the theory appeared Tuesday on the website of Bill O'Reilly, the ousted Fox News host. Mr. O'Reilly stopped short of saying the students had been planted by anti-Trump forces. But, he wrote: "The national press believes it is their job to destroy the Trump administration by any means necessary. So if the media has to use kids to do that, they'll use kids."

Some of those who have been spreading the conspiracies are facing consequences.

Benjamin Kelly, an aide to a Florida state representative, Shawn Harrison, emailed a Tampa Bay Times reporter on Tuesday accusing Mr. Hogg and a classmate, Emma Gonzalez, of being actors that travel to the sites of crises.

Mr. Kelly was soon fired.

"I made a mistake whereas I tried to inform a reporter of information relating to his story regarding a school shooting," Mr. Kelly tweeted. "I meant no disrespect to the students or parents of Parkland." His boss, Mr. Harrison, said on Twitter that he was "appalled" by Mr. Kelly's remarks.

But by Tuesday evening, a new conspiracy was dominating Gateway Pundit's home page. "Soros-Linked Organizers of 'Women's March' Selected Anti-Trump Kids to Be Face of Parkland Tragedy," read the headline. Within an hour, it had been shared on Facebook more than 150 times.

The Making of a No. 1 YouTube Conspiracy Video After the Parkland Tragedy

BY JOHN HERRMAN | FEB. 21, 2018

YOUTUBE'S LIST OF "Trending" videos typically includes funny clips, updates from popular YouTube personalities, movie trailers and viral TV segments. On Wednesday, for a brief time, the No. 1 trending video on YouTube featured David Hogg, a survivor of the massacre last week at Marjory Stoneman Douglas High School in Parkland, Fla.

The caption claimed, falsely, that Mr. Hogg, 17, was not a student, but an "actor."

SAUL MARTINEZ FOR THE NEW YORK TIMES

David Hogg, 17, has become a prominent student voice since the shooting at Marjory Stoneman Douglas High School in Parkland, Fla. A YouTube video that rose to the top trending spot on the service accused him of being an actor.

The video, originally posted last August, was a brief local news segment. In it, Mr. Hogg was interviewed by the CBS affiliate in Los Angeles after witnessing a dispute between a lifeguard and a swimmer at Redondo Beach.

On Tuesday, a YouTube user who went under the name "mike m." copied and re-uploaded the video with a new caption: "DAVID HOGG THE ACTOR...."

With that terse descriptor, "mike m." tapped into conspiracies circulating online that the survivors of the Parkland shooting, many of whom have recently spoken out in favor of gun control, were "crisis actors" hired to do the bidding of left-wing activists.

The reposted video moved its way up the trending list overnight. By Wednesday morning, it had accumulated more than 200,000 views.

"I had no idea where all the attention was coming from," said "mike m." in an online chat interview with The New York Times. "I just noticed it started to take off."

Many commenters were confused. "Why is this on trending, especially on news? Nothing special," wrote one. Others, tipped off by the caption calling Mr. Hogg an actor, knew exactly what they thought they were seeing: "Someone get this kid an Oscar!" one wrote.

By noon on Wednesday, YouTube had pulled the video for violating its policy on harassment and bullying.

It was not the first time that YouTube had served not just as a source of fringe conspiracy theories, but as an accomplice in their rapid spread.

After the massacre in Las Vegas last October, YouTubers filled a void of information about the killer's motives with dark speculation, crowding the site with videos that were fonts of discredited and unproven information, including claims that the tragedy had been staged.

After a mass shooting last November at a church in Sutherland Springs, Tex., those seeking news about the event on YouTube were overwhelmed by videos falsely claiming it had been a "false flag" attack meant to spur gun control measures or a plot carried out by the so-called antifa (short for anti-fascist) movement.

In the wake of this latest tragedy, which left 17 people dead at the school in Parkland, YouTube still seemed caught by surprise by the rise of another video meant to peddle a baseless theory.

"In 2017, we started rolling out changes to better surface authoritative news sources in search results, particularly around breaking news events," YouTube, which is owned by Google, said in a statement. "We've seen improvements, but in some circumstances these changes are not working quickly enough. In addition, last year we updated the application of our harassment policy to include hoax videos that target the victims of these tragedies."

Unlike the other unhinged clips that have garnered significant attention on YouTube in the recent past, the video of the Parkland survivor originated with neither a conspiracy-oriented media organization like Infowars nor one of the popular YouTubers who have catered to far-right subcultures and fringe political factions.

Instead, it was posted to the infrequently updated account run by "mike m." Up until the reposting of the video featuring Mr. Hogg, the account had fewer than a dozen videos and fewer than 1,000 followers. Although he declined to provide much information about himself or give his full name, "mike m." said that he was a 51-year-old man living in Idaho.

His uploads included a handful of little-watched videos suggesting he is an avid fan of conspiracies. What inspired him to traffic in an unfounded theory about the Parkland shooting — aside from "having more time on my hands these days," he said — were posts he had seen on the popular conspiracy site Godlike Productions. He pointed to comments on the site that claimed Mr. Hogg had been "coached" before giving interviews to members of the media who covered the massacre. It's also where he found references to the beach video from last August.

Speaking to CNN on Tuesday, Mr. Hogg addressed the explosion of conspiracy theories head-on. "I'm not a crisis actor," said Mr. Hogg, who had been visiting family and friends when he appeared in the Los Angeles news segment. "I'm someone who had to witness this and live through this and I continue to be having to do that. I'm not acting on anybody's behalf."

The video posted by "mike m." rapidly gained steam nonetheless.

What propelled this one to popularity — and eventually into YouTube's promotional apparatus — came from outside the platform.

Links to the video proliferated on 4chan, where users have gleefully embraced the conspiracy theories and mocked the shooting victims. When it hit YouTube's Trending page, some on 4chan celebrated: "TRENDING IN THE USA," began one thread in the far-right politics board called /pol/. "WE'RE BREAKING THE CONDITIONING."

The "mike m." video also found traction on Twitter, on Facebook and in stories and comment threads on conspiracy sites. It rose in the circuitous and unexpected manner of a viral video, rather than one that had been calculated to game YouTube's algorithms by seizing on interest in breaking news or tragedy — it had no catchy headline, no recognizable personality, no vast theorizing. And yet it blasted through YouTube's safeguards and somehow kept going, exposing the platform as vulnerable to sudden influence from inside and outside its walls.

After YouTube removed the video, "mike m." said his account had received a "strike" — that is how YouTube warns users that they have broken the site's rules or violated its guidelines. (Three strikes and you're out.) "I mean, why strike me over a beach confrontation video???" he said. A second video he had posted about the shooting was gaining popularity Wednesday morning, he said, until it, too, was deleted, and another strike was added to his account.

Anonymous and remorseless, "mike m." was undeterred. "There is more to this kid than appears on MSM," he said, using the common shorthand for "mainstream media." Asked if he would think twice about posting such videos in the future, he said, "No not at all."

He said he was worried about his account getting deleted, adding: "But I am not going to stop."

After Florida School Shooting, Russian 'Bot' Army Pounced

BY SHEERA FRENKEL AND DAISUKE WAKABAYASHI | FEB. 19, 2018

SAN FRANCISCO — One hour after news broke about the school shooting in Florida last week, Twitter accounts suspected of having links to Russia released hundreds of posts taking up the gun control debate.

The accounts addressed the news with the speed of a cable news network. Some adopted the hashtag #guncontrolnow. Others used #gunreformnow and #Parklandshooting. Earlier on Wednesday, before the mass shooting at Marjory Stoneman Douglas High School in Parkland, Fla., many of those accounts had been focused on the investigation by the special counsel Robert S. Mueller III into Russian meddling in the 2016 presidential election.

"This is pretty typical for them, to hop on breaking news like this," said Jonathon Morgan, chief executive of New Knowledge, a company that tracks online disinformation campaigns. "The bots focus on anything that is divisive for Americans. Almost systematically."

One of the most divisive issues in the nation is how to handle guns, pitting Second Amendment advocates against proponents of gun control. And the messages from these automated accounts, or bots, were designed to widen the divide and make compromise even more difficult.

Any news event — no matter how tragic — has become fodder to spread inflammatory messages in what is believed to be a far-reaching Russian disinformation campaign. The disinformation comes in various forms: conspiracy videos on YouTube, fake interest groups on Facebook, and armies of bot accounts that can hijack a topic or discussion on Twitter.

Those automated Twitter accounts have been closely tracked by researchers. Last year, the Alliance for Securing Democracy, in conjunction with the German Marshall Fund, a public policy research

SAUL MARTINEZ FOR THE NEW YORK TIMES

A weekend gun control rally in Fort Lauderdale, Fla. One hour after news of the school shooting in nearby Parkland spread, Twitter accounts that researchers have linked to Russia shifted their focus to the gun control debate.

group in Washington, created a website that tracks hundreds of Twitter accounts of human users and suspected bots that they have linked to a Russian influence campaign.

The researchers zeroed in on Twitter accounts posting information that was in step with material coming from well-known Russian propaganda outlets. To spot an automated bot, they looked for certain signs, like an extremely high volume of posts or content that conspicuously matched hundreds of other accounts.

The researchers said they had watched as the bots began posting about the Parkland shooting shortly after it happened.

Amplified by bot swarms, Russian-linked Twitter accounts tried to foment discord before and after the election. Hundreds of accounts promoted false stories about Hillary Clinton and spread articles based on leaked emails from Democratic operatives that had been obtained by Russian hackers.

Facebook, Google and Twitter have, to varying degrees, announced new measures to eliminate bot accounts, and have hired more moderators to help them weed out disinformation on their platforms.

But since the election, the Russian-linked bots have rallied around other divisive issues, often ones that President Trump has tweeted about. They promoted Twitter hashtags like #boycottnfl, #standforouranthem and #takeaknee after some National Football League players started kneeling during the national anthem to protest racial injustice.

The automated Twitter accounts helped popularize the #releasethememo hashtag, which referred to a secret House Republican memorandum that suggested the F.B.I. and the Justice Department abused their authority to obtain a warrant to spy on a former Trump campaign adviser. The debate over the memo widened a schism between the White House and its own law enforcement agencies.

The bots are "going to find any contentious issue, and instead of making it an opportunity for compromise and negotiation, they turn it into an unsolvable issue bubbling with frustration," said Karen North, a social media professor at the University of Southern California's Annenberg School for Communication and Journalism. "It just heightens that frustration and anger."

Intelligence officials in the United States have warned that malicious actors will try to spread disinformation ahead of the 2018 midterm elections. In testimony to Congress last year and in private meetings with lawmakers, social media companies promised that they will do better in 2018 than they did in 2016.

But the Twitter campaign around the Parkland shooting is an example of how Russian operatives are still at it.

"We've had more than a year to get our act together and address the threat posed by Russia and implement a strategy to deter future attacks, but I believe, unfortunately, we still don't have a comprehensive plan," said Senator Mark Warner, the Virginia Democrat who is the vice chairman of the Senate Intelligence Committee, during a hearing this month on global threats to the United States. "What we're seeing is a continuous assault by Russia to target and undermine our democratic institutions, and they're going to keep coming at us."

When the Russian bots jumped on the hashtag #Parklandshooting — initially created to spread news of the shooting — they quickly stoked tensions. Exploiting the issue of mental illness in the gun control debate, they propagated the notion that Nikolas Cruz, the suspected gunman, was a mentally ill "lone killer." They also claimed that he had searched for Arabic phrases on Google before the shooting. Simultaneously, the bots started other hashtags, like #ar15, for the semiautomatic rifle used in the shooting, and #NRA.

The bots' behavior follows a pattern, said Mr. Morgan, one of the researchers who worked with the German Marshall Fund to create Hamilton 68, the website that monitors Russian bot and fake Twitter activity. The bots target a contentious issue like race relations or guns. They stir the pot, often animating both sides and creating public doubt in institutions like the police or media. Any issue associated with extremist views is a ripe target.

The goal is to push fringe ideas into the "slightly more mainstream," Mr. Morgan said. If well-known people retweet the bot messages or simply link to a website the bots are promoting, the messages gain an edge of legitimacy.

An indictment made public on Friday by Mr. Mueller as part of the investigation into Russian interference in the election mentioned a Russian Twitter feed, @TEN_GOP, which posed as a Tennessee Republican account and attracted more than 100,000 followers. Messages from this now-deleted account were retweeted by the president's sons and close advisers including Kellyanne Conway and Michael T. Flynn, the former national security adviser.

The indictment also described how fraudulent Russian accounts on Twitter tried to push real Americans into action. The indictment said the fake Twitter account @March_for_Trump had organized political rallies for Mr. Trump in New York before the election, including a

"March for Trump" rally on June 25, 2016, and a "Down With Hillary" gathering on July 23, 2016.

By Friday morning, the bots that pushed the original tweets around the Parkland shooting had moved on to the hashtag #falseflag — a term used by conspiracy theorists to refer to a secret government operation that is carried out to look like something else — with a conspiracy theory that the shooting had never happened.

By Monday, the bots had new targets: the Daytona 500 auto race in Daytona Beach, Fla., and news about William Holleeder, a man facing trial in the Netherlands for his suspected role in six gangland killings. It is unclear why.

Facebook and Google Struggle to Squelch 'Crisis Actor' Posts

BY JACK NICAS AND SHEERA FRENKEL | FEB. 23, 2018

SAN FRANCISCO — On Wednesday, one week after the school shooting in Parkland, Fla., Facebook and YouTube vowed to crack down on the trolls.

Thousands of posts and videos had popped up on the sites, falsely claiming that survivors of the shooting were paid actors or part of various conspiracy theories. Facebook called the posts "abhorrent." YouTube, which is owned by Google, said it needed to do better. Both promised to remove the content.

The companies have since aggressively pulled down many posts and videos and reduced the visibility of others. Yet on Friday, spot searches of the sites revealed that the noxious content was far from eradicated.

On Facebook and Instagram, which is owned by Facebook, searches for the hashtag #crisisactor, which accused the Parkland survivors of being actors, turned up hundreds of posts perpetuating the falsehood (though some also criticized the conspiracy theory). Many of the posts had been tweaked ever so slightly — for example, videos had been renamed #propaganda rather than #hoax — to evade automated detection. And on YouTube, while many of the conspiracy videos claiming that the students were actors had been taken down, other videos that claimed the shooting had been a hoax remained rife.

Facebook faced renewed criticism on Friday after it was revealed that the company showcased a virtual reality shooting game at the Conservative Political Action Conference this week. Facebook said it was removing the game from its demonstration of its new virtual reality products.

The resilience of misinformation, despite efforts by the tech behemoths to eliminate it, has become a real-time case study of how the companies are constantly a step behind in stamping out the content. At every turn, trolls, conspiracy theorists and others have proved to be more adept at taking advantage of exactly what the sites were created to do — encourage people to post almost anything they want — than the companies are at catching them.

"They're not able to police their platforms when the type of content that they're promising to prohibit changes on a too-frequent basis," Jonathon Morgan, founder of New Knowledge, a company that tracks disinformation online, said of Facebook and YouTube.

The difficulty of dealing with inappropriate online content stands out with the Parkland shooting because the tech companies have effectively committed to removing any accusations that the Parkland survivors were actors, a step they did not take after other recent mass shootings, such as last October's massacre in Las Vegas. In the past, the companies typically addressed specific types of content only when it was illegal — posts from terrorist organizations, for example — Mr. Morgan said.

Facebook and YouTube's promises follow a stream of criticism in recent months over how their sites can be gamed to spread Russian propaganda, among other abuses. The companies have said they are betting big on artificial intelligence systems to help identify and take down inappropriate content, though that technology is still being developed.

The companies have in the meantime hired or said they plan to hire more people to comb through what is posted to their sites. Facebook said it was hiring 1,000 new moderators to review content and was making changes to what type of news publishers would be favored on the social network. YouTube has said that it plans to have 10,000 moderators by year's end and that it is altering its search algorithms to return more videos from reliable news sources.

Mary deBree, head of content policy at Facebook, said the company had not been perfect at staving off certain content and most likely would not be in the future.

"False information is like any other challenge where humans are involved: It evolves, much like a rumor or urban legend would. It also masks itself as legitimate speech," she said. "Our job is to do better at keeping this bad content off Facebook without undermining the reason people come here — to see things happening in the world around them and have a conversation about them."

A YouTube spokeswoman said in a statement that the site updated its harassment policy last year "to include hoax videos that target the victims of these tragedies. Any video flagged to us that violates this policy is reviewed and then removed."

For many people, getting around Facebook and YouTube's hunt to remove noxious content is straightforward. The sites have automated detection systems that often search for specific terms or images that have previously been deemed unacceptable. So to evade those systems, people sometimes can alter images or switch to different terminology.

Sam Woolley, an internet researcher at the nonprofit Institute for the Future, said far-right groups had started using internet brands to describe minorities — like "Skype" to indicate Jewish people — to trick software and human reviewers.

Those who post conspiracy theories also tend to quickly repost or engage with similar posts from other accounts, creating a sort of viral effect that can cause the sites' algorithms to promote the content as a trending topic or a recommended video, said David Carroll, a professor at the New School who studies tech platforms.

That duplication and repackaging of misinformation "make the game of snuffing it out Whac-a-Mole to the extreme," he said.

That game played out across the web in the past few days, after a video suggesting that one of the most vocal Parkland survivors, David Hogg, was an actor became the No. 1 trending video on YouTube. After a public outcry, YouTube removed the video and said it would take down other "crisis actor" videos because they violated its ban on bullying. YouTube has since scrubbed its site of many such videos.

Yet some of the videos remained, possibly because they used slightly different terminology. One clip that had drawn more than 77,000 views by Friday described the shooting survivors as "disaster performers" instead of "crisis actors."

Other videos that were not about the Parkland survivors but that called the entire shooting into question also stayed online. A video posted last week by Alex Jones, the founder of the conspiracy theory site Infowars, titled "Red Alert! Evidence Mounts Florida Attacks Is a Giant False Flag" had attracted more than 300,000 views by Friday.

On Facebook, some of the posts the social network had vowed to ban were still gaining traction. One lengthy post had been shared more than 3,800 times by early Friday. The post included a photo of Mr. Hogg and his classmate Emma Gonzalez with the text "Globalist Deep State Crisis Actors."

After The New York Times contacted the author of the post, a self-described political analyst named John Miranda, the post disappeared. It is unclear if Facebook removed it. Mr. Miranda did not respond to a request for comment.

The tech companies' increasing efforts to remove misinformation have a side effect: angering some of their most active users.

Moe Othman, a comedian and commentator on YouTube who has about 60,000 subscribers, said that within 10 minutes of posting a video on Wednesday that suggested some Parkland students were actors, YouTube removed it and placed a strike on his account. YouTube terminates accounts after three strikes.

Mr. Othman said in a private message on Twitter: "I'm not surprised. We live in a world where information is one of the most important tools." He added, "In this case, I see YouTube as a censoring machine."

Would he stop using YouTube? No, he said, "mainly because I'm still a comedian who simply wants to make people laugh."

YouTube Cracks Down on Far-Right Videos as Conspiracy Theories Spread

BY JONAH ENGEL BROMWICH | MARCH 3, 2018

YOUTUBE THIS WEEK cracked down on the videos of some prominent far-right actors and conspiracy theorists, continuing an effort that has become more visible since the school shooting in Parkland, Fla., last month caused a torrent of misinformation to be featured prominently on the site.

A week after the shooting, many of the videos on YouTube's "Trending" list contained misinformation about the teenage survivors of the shooting. The top video on the list for some time falsely claimed that a student at the school, David Hogg, was a paid actor.

That video and others like it led to intense criticism of the site. Since then, many prominent right-wing personalities have reported that YouTube has issued them strikes, which the site uses to enforce its community guidelines. If a channel receives three strikes within three months, YouTube terminates it.

The company's guidelines prohibit "videos that contain nudity or sexual content, violent or graphic content, harmful or dangerous content, hateful content, threats, spam, misleading metadata, or scams."

Mike Cernovich, the right-wing agitator and conspiracy theorist, said Wednesday that his channel, which has more than 66,000 subscribers, had been given a strike. (Mr. Cernovich said Saturday that YouTube had reversed the strike and that the video that had been banned was again available on the site.)

Infowars, the conspiracy theory outlet headed by Alex Jones, said Tuesday that it had received a second strike in two weeks, both for videos about the Parkland shooting. (Infowars, which has more than 2.2 million YouTube subscribers, later said the second strike had been removed.) Infowars' Washington bureau chief, Jerome Corsi, said on

Twitter that his YouTube channel had been terminated without notice or explanation.

News outlets including The Outline and Breitbart have pointed to more than a dozen other right-wing or right-leaning accounts that have been disciplined, claiming they have either received strikes or been banned outright in the past several weeks.

They include the violent neo-Nazi group Atomwaffen (banned for hate speech) and the YouTube star Carl Benjamin, known by his username Sargon of Akkad, who criticizes feminism and identity politics. Mr. Benjamin posted a screenshot on Facebook on Thursday that said he had been locked out of his Google account because "it looked like it was being used in a way that violated Google's policies."

YouTube said it was not aware of any prominent accounts that had falsely reported strikes, though it did say that Mr. Benjamin had violated its policy on copyright infringement.

YouTube denied that the deletions and other actions were ideologically driven. It said accounts that had been disciplined or banned were only the most prominent, and vocal, of many across the ideological spectrum who had seen their videos taken down for violating the site's rules.

But critics said YouTube was reacting haphazardly in an attempt to purge actors who have garnered it negative attention. They questioned whether the site was prepared to substantively address the problem of the conspiracy theories that flourish on its platform.

And some of the right-wing YouTube stars and conspiracists who were affected saw the disciplinary action as a result of what they say is left-wing ideology flourishing inside Google, of which YouTube is a subsidiary. Mr. Benjamin told Breitbart that the company was "riddled with a far-left ideological orthodoxy that has taken hold to a radical degree."

A YouTube spokeswoman said in a statement that its "reviewers remove content according to our policies, not according to politics or ideology, and we use quality control measures to ensure they are applying our policies without bias."

The company is in the middle of hiring a large influx of moderators, and it attributed some of its recent enforcement actions to a group who are still learning to apply its rules.

"With the volume of videos on our platform, sometimes we make mistakes and when this is brought to our attention we reinstate videos or channels that were incorrectly removed," the company's statement said.

The moderation efforts of YouTube, like those of Facebook and Twitter, have begun to receive more attention in the last year as academics and journalists have focused on how misinformation — like that sown by Russia during the 2016 presidential election — is spread.

In a December blog post, YouTube announced it would add many people to its work force in 2018, hoping eventually to have 10,000 working to moderate or otherwise address content that has violated its rules.

The company is in the process of hiring many of those people. A spokeswoman said that applying the company's standards to any given video required training, and that new moderators were bound to make some mistakes. It said that some of the strikes that had been handed out since the Parkland shooting had been mistaken, though it did not specify which.

Jonathan Albright, the research director of the Tow Center for Digital Journalism and an expert on how misinformation thrives on social media, said YouTube has long been inconsistent in its enforcement of its guidelines.

"If these accounts are getting deleted at the last minute because people are angry and news organizations are digging into this, should these accounts have existed in the first place?" he asked.

Negative news media attention results in more users flagging videos of right-wing conspiracy theorists, leading to a feedback loop in which channels promoting those views are disciplined. The effect is that its disciplinary process is reactive, and relies on users to flag content they find troublesome.

A YouTube spokeswoman said the company planned to release a transparency report in the spring that it says will show the full range of videos that have been taken down.

Zack Exley, a left-wing populist who runs the YouTube channel Left Right Forward, said that the bans of high-profile right-wing accounts may do more harm than good by building up the reputations of extremists among their bases.

"The extreme right loves being censored," he said. "They become heroes and raise tons of money every time YouTube removes or demonetizes their videos."

YouTube does not police misinformation, which, on its own, does not violate the site's guidelines. But the company says it is confident that, with its steep increase in moderators and progress in machine learning, it will be capable of enforcing its rules effectively, which will help stem the tide of objectionable videos.

Mr. Albright said that hiring many more people would help. But he said that those people would have to be trained to address difficult situations, applying the platform's rules to nuanced videos in which the right decision was not always clear.

"It would take a group of people specifically trained in this kind of situation," he said. "It's a problem of scale. This stuff doesn't scale like algorithms. Humans don't scale."

"YouTube isn't in a 'too big to fail' situation," he added. "But they're potentially too big to moderate."

Alex Jones, Pursued Over Infowars Falsehoods, Faces a Legal Crossroads

BY ELIZABETH WILLIAMSON | JULY 31, 2018

AUSTIN, TEX. — In the five years since Noah Pozner was killed at Sandy Hook Elementary School in Newtown, Conn., death threats and online harassment have forced his parents, Veronique De La Rosa and Leonard Pozner, to relocate seven times. They now live in a high-security community hundreds of miles from where their 6-year-old is buried.

"I would love to go see my son's grave and I don't get to do that, but we made the right decision," Ms. De La Rosa said in a recent interview. Each time they have moved, online fabulists stalking the family have published their whereabouts.

"With the speed of light," she said. "They have their own community, and they have the ear of some very powerful people."

On Wednesday in an Austin courtroom, the struggle of the Sandy Hook families to hold to account Alex Jones, a powerful leader of this online community, will reach a crossroads. Lawyers for Noah Pozner's parents will seek to convince a Texas judge that they — and by extension the families of eight other victims in the 2012 shooting that killed 20 first graders and six adults — have a valid defamation claim against Mr. Jones, whose Austin-based Infowars media operation spread false claims that the shooting was an elaborate hoax.

The Pozner hearing is a bellwether in three cases, including another in Texas and one in Connecticut, filed by relatives of nine Sandy Hook victims. It comes as the social media platforms Mr. Jones relies upon to spread incendiary claims initiate efforts to curb him.

The day after the Pozner case, in the same courthouse, is a hearing in a separate defamation case against Mr. Jones brought by Marcel Fontaine, who was falsely identified on Infowars' website as the gunman in

ILANA PANICH-LINSMAN FOR THE NEW YORK TIMES

Alex Jones is being sued over Infowars' spread of false claims that the 2012 shooting at Sandy Hook Elementary School in Newtown, Conn., was an elaborate hoax.

the Parkland, Fla., school shooting in February. Mr. Fontaine, who lives in Massachusetts, has never visited Florida. The Pozner family and Mr. Fontaine are being represented by Mark Bankston of Farrar & Ball, a law firm based in Houston.

Mr. Jones is trying to have the Pozner and Fontaine cases dismissed under the Texas Citizens Participation Act, which protects citizens' right to free speech against plaintiffs who aim to silence them through costly litigation. Mr. Jones is seeking more than $100,000 in court costs from the Pozner family. Efforts to reach Mr. Jones on his cellphone and through the Infowars email were unsuccessful. Mark Enoch, his lawyer in the case, did not respond to telephone and email requests for comment.

Mr. Jones has emerged as an avatar for a "post truth" ethos that flourished online during the last presidential campaign. He gained a national spotlight and millions of followers after Donald J. Trump appeared on his show during the campaign, praising his reputation as "amazing." Since then, many of Mr. Jones's bogus theories have targeted President Trump's perceived adversaries and reflect opinions held by his political base.

Last week Mr. Jones broadcast a bizarre accusation that Robert S. Mueller III, the special counsel investigating Russian interference in the 2016 election, was involved in a child sex ring. In an online broadcast, Mr. Jones addressed Mr. Mueller while repeatedly imitating firing a handgun, saying: "It's the real world. Politically. You're going to get it, or I'm going to die trying."

Recent "most popular" stories on the Infowars website included "Marine Veteran, Man Wearing Trump Shirt Violently Attacked Near Trump Star in L.A.," "Revealed: U.N. Plan to Flood America With 600 Million Migrants," and "Left Protests 'Racist' Stand Your Ground Law After Black Man Shot in Self-Defense."

On Friday, Facebook removed Mr. Jones's personal page from the site for 30 days, citing "bullying" and "hate speech." The company has yet to take any action against the Infowars Facebook page, despite pleas from Sandy Hook parents. Last week, YouTube removed four of Mr. Jones's videos for violating its child endangerment and hate speech standards and barred him from live-streaming on the site for 90 days, though his channel remains a main source for his broadcasts.

The videos removed included one called "Prevent Liberalism," in which a man chokes a child and throws him to the ground. Another one was called "Shock Report: Learn How Islam Has Already Conquered Europe."

Mr. Jones and his lawyers say in court filings that the Pozner family's suit is an effort "to silence those who openly oppose their very public 'herculean' efforts to ban the sale of certain weapons, ammunition and accessories, to pass new laws relating to gun registration and to limit free speech."

That stance echoes Mr. Jones's original false claims that Sandy Hook was staged by government-backed gun control activists. Mr. Jones's lawyer says in court filings that Mr. Jones's theories are opinion, which is more broadly protected by the First Amendment. He also maintains that Mr. Pozner and Ms. De La Rosa are public figures, because Mr. Pozner has created a nonprofit to combat the harm caused by online falsehoods and Ms. De La Rosa has advocated a ban on assault weapons, like the AR-15-style rifle used in the Sandy Hook shooting.

If the parents are found to be public figures, they will have to prove actual malice, or that Mr. Jones knew the claims were false, but repeated them anyway.

The Pozner family's story is recounted in the court filings: In 2015, after Mr. Pozner succeeded in having an Infowars video taken down from Mr. Jones's YouTube channel, "Mr. Jones went on an angry rant about me for nearly an hour," Mr. Pozner said in an affidavit. Mr. Jones "also hosted a call with an obsessed fellow conspiracy theorist who issued a threat to me."

"Mr. Jones then showed his audience my personal information and maps to addresses associated with my family," the affidavit says.

Lucy Richards, an Infowars devotee, was arrested the next year for repeatedly threatening Mr. Pozner's life. She was sentenced to five months in prison last year. As a condition of parole, a judge ordered that she cease consuming Infowars programming, the court documents state.

"This type of misinformation is a bit of a societal crisis," Ms. De La Rosa said. "This isn't someone on a soapbox in Times Square spewing nonsense. It's someone who every day generates income from his demonstrably false utterances."

Starting days after the shooting, Mr. Jones helped spread false claims that the Sandy Hook parents were "crisis actors" in a government conspiracy. A month after the shooting, he began broadcasting excerpts from Ms. De La Rosa's interview with the CNN anchor Anderson Cooper, which was taped in front of the Edmond Town Hall in Newtown. Mr. Jones falsely claimed that the interview was taped in a studio before a "green screen."

In an April 2017 Infowars broadcast titled "Sandy Hook Vampires Exposed," according to the court documents, Mr. Jones aired the clip of Ms. De La Rosa's interview, noting that when Mr. Cooper turns his head, "his nose disappears repeatedly because the green screen isn't set right." The Pozner filings include an affidavit from Grant Fredericks, a forensic video analyst and expert witness, in which he attributes the anomaly in the videotape to "postproduction compression," common in video production, and said "no credible video professional, editor or web-content specialist would conclude" that the interview was taped in front of a screen.

In court filings responding to the Pozner suit, Mr. Jones's lawyer says that "certain comments that he had previously made in connection with possible faking or staging events at the Sandy Hook shooting was not an accusation against the children or families, but against the media and government officials, whose actions led many to question the official version of the event." The parents, the filing says, "isolate specific statements, take them out of context while ignoring other relevant portions, and misinterpret what was said."

Ms. De La Rosa and Mr. Pozner will not appear in court on Wednesday, in part because of safety concerns.

Conspiracy Theories Made Alex Jones Very Rich. They May Bring Him Down.

BY ELIZABETH WILLIAMSON AND EMILY STEEL | SEPT. 7, 2018

AUSTIN — More than ever before in his two-decade career built on baseless conspiracy theories, angry nativist rants and end-of-days fearmongering, Alex Jones is being called to account.

In a Texas courthouse, his lawyers are battling defamation claims resulting from one of his most infamous acts: spreading false reports that the Sandy Hook massacre of 20 first graders and six adults was an elaborate hoax.

In Silicon Valley, Facebook, YouTube and, as of Thursday, Twitter, under pressure to better curb hate speech and incendiary misinformation, have largely cut him off. On Friday, Apple removed the Infowars app from its App Store, eliminating one of the final avenues for Mr. Jones to reach a mainstream audience.

Mr. Jones's latest stunt — turning up on Capitol Hill this week to call attention to his claim that he is being unfairly silenced on ideological grounds — led to an embarrassing rebuff by a conservative Republican senator.

The big question for him now is whether his bluster — and the implicit support he has received from President Trump, who has channeled bogus or misleading claims promoted by Mr. Jones and echoed his complaints of anticonservatism by technology companies — will be sufficient to see him past his current peril. He is facing a legal, public opinion and social media reckoning that poses the most serious threat yet not just to his ability to inject the outlandish into the mainstream, but also to the lucrative business he has built.

Mr. Jones likes to portray his digital channel, Infowars, as a media outlet, and he is quick to wrap himself in the First Amendment. But in business terms, it is more accurate to describe Infowars as an online store that uses Mr. Jones's commentary to move merchandise. Its revenue comes primarily from the sale of a grab-bag of health-enhancement and survivalist products that Mr. Jones hawks constantly.

A close look at his career shows that he has been as much a canny if unconventional entrepreneur as an ideological agitator. He has adapted to — and profited from — changes in both the political climate and the media business even as he has tested, and regularly crossed, the boundaries of acceptable public discourse.

For more than two decades, Mr. Jones, who is 44, has built a substantial following appealing to an angry, largely white, majority male audience that can choose simply to be entertained or to internalize his rendering of their worst fears: that the government and other big institutions are out to get them, that some form of apocalypse is frighteningly close and that they must become more virile, and better-armed, to survive.

ERIC THAYER FOR THE NEW YORK TIMES

Alex Jones spoke to the media on Tuesday as officials from Facebook and Twitter testified on Capitol Hill.

“I’m not a business guy, I’m a revolutionary,” he said in an interview in August.

If it is a revolution, it is one that he has skillfully monetized. His fundamental insight was that his audience is also a nearly captive market for the variety of goods he peddles via Infowars’ website and his syndicated radio show — products intended to assuage the same fears he stokes.

Infowars and its affiliated companies are private and do not have to report financial results publicly. But by 2014, according to testimony Mr. Jones gave in a court case, his operations were bringing in more than $20 million a year in revenue. Records viewed by The New York Times show that most of his revenue that year came from the sale of products like supplements such as the Super Male Vitality, which purports to boost testosterone, or Brain Force Plus, which promises to “supercharge” cognitive functions.

Court records in a divorce case show that Mr. Jones’s businesses netted more than $5 million in 2014. Court proceedings show that he and his then-wife, Kelly Jones, embarked on plans to build a swimming pool complex around that time featuring a waterfall and dining cabana with a stone fireplace. Mr. Jones bought four Rolex watches in one day in 2014, and spent $40,000 on a saltwater aquarium; the couple’s assets at the time included a $70,000 grand piano, $50,000 in firearms and $752,000 in silver, gold and precious metals, in a safe deposit box, court documents say.

People who have worked with him or studied his business said his revenues had probably continued to grow in recent years.

But his problems are mounting. At least five defamation suits against Mr. Jones, including three filed by Sandy Hook families, are moving forward. Last month, a Texas judge ordered Mr. Jones and officers in his web of limited-liability companies to provide depositions to lawyers for the parent of a Sandy Hook victim in coming weeks, testimony that could shed new light on Mr. Jones’s operation.

He is also facing complaints of workplace discrimination from two ex-employees, a fraud and product liability case and a nasty court battle with Ms. Jones, now his ex-wife. She says that the couple have spent a combined $4 million on their four-year battle over custody of their three children and disputes over the business.

At the same time, the crackdown on Mr. Jones in August by the social media giants — he has been largely banned by Facebook, YouTube, Apple, Spotify and even Pinterest — poses a severe test by limiting his access to his audience. The early evidence is that the bans have substantially reduced his reach — and that was before a double blow this week when Twitter imposed a permanent ban on his account and the account for Infowars and Apple removed the Infowars app from its store.

Apple had already removed Mr. Jones's show from its podcast service on Aug. 5. On Friday, an Apple spokeswoman said the app was removed under company policies that prohibit apps from including content that is "offensive, insensitive, upsetting, intended to disgust, or in exceptionally poor taste."

Mr. Jones will be forced to rely even more on his Infowars site and his radio show, which is heard on more than 100 stations nationwide.

True to form, Mr. Jones is using the challenge to move more product.

For several days in August, after the ban by the social media companies, his online Infowars Store offered deep discounts under an all-caps banner that read, "FIGHT THE BULLIES, SAVE THE INTERNET, SAVE INFOWARS."

The best-selling Survival Shield X-2 nascent iodine drops were discounted 40 percent, to $23.95, while Alpha Power, a product marketed as boosting testosterone and vitality to "push back in the fight against the globalist agenda," was half off, at $34.95.

"The enemy wants to cut off our funding to destroy us," Mr. Jones said on his broadcast, concluding a segment about being banned by the social media companies with a sales pitch for another product. "If you don't fund us, we'll be shut down."

ILANA PANICH-LINSMAN FOR THE NEW YORK TIMES

Mr. Jones in the Infowars studio.

Mr. Jones operates from behind bulletproof glass at an Austin industrial park, in a dimly lit hive of studios and cluttered, open-plan desks. He invited a New York Times reporter there for an interview on two conditions: that the location of his headquarters not be specified and that he would record audio of the interview.

There are no identifying signs outside. Inside, there are split-screen security camera monitors throughout, which Mr. Jones checks as he passes by. There are guns in the building for protection, he said. He added that armed snipers are positioned on the roof, then in a phone call the next day said that he had made that up. He wouldn't say how many employees he has, but in 2017 court testimony he said he employed 75 people, plus 10 contractors.

Mr. Jones talked for nearly three hours, bouncing around the room, raising his voice, feigning menace, replaying themes and entire riffs from his show.

"I am here giving you the unfiltered truth of my soul," he said.

He insisted that his troubles are proof that a globalist, leftist cabal aims to silence him.

He claimed advance knowledge that technology companies, Chinese communists, Democrats and the mainstream media would "try to use me as a 2018, 2020 campaign issue — to hurt Trump, to misrepresent what I've said, to project it on Trump, and to go after the First Amendment and legitimize the censorship of all the Republican congresspeople."

It was classic Alex Jones: a nonstop mix of flimsy fact, grievance, paranoia, ideology, combativeness and solipsism.

Mr. Jones often exhorts his listeners to "investigate" the hoaxes and theories he advances, pleas that may have inspired criminal acts by some of his followers.

In 2000, Mr. Jones and his cameraman, Mike Hanson, infiltrated Bohemian Grove, an annual camping retreat for global business and political leaders near Monte Rio, Calif. The pair shot dim video of a pyrotechnic spectacle that Mr. Jones wrongly claimed was an "occult ritual."

Early in 2002, a heavily armed man entered the grounds and set a fire. Citing Mr. Jones's reports, he said he was convinced that child abuse and human sacrifices were taking place at the retreat.

A similar scenario unfolded more than a decade later, when during the 2016 campaign Mr. Jones helped spread the "Pizzagate" hoax, that Hillary Clinton and Democratic operatives were running a child sex ring from a pizzeria in Washington, D.C.

An Infowars listener, Edgar Maddison Welch, entered the pizzeria in late 2016 armed with a military-style rifle to investigate and rescue children he believed were being held captive, firing the gun inside the restaurant as patrons fled. He is serving a four-year jail term.

Mr. Jones for years spread the false claim that the Sandy Hook shooting was a fraud, and that the victims' relatives were actors in a hoax planned by government "gun grabbers."

In 2015, after Leonard Pozner, whose son Noah died at Sandy Hook, got one of Mr. Jones's Sandy Hook hoax broadcasts removed from YouTube, Mr. Jones showed viewers Mr. Pozner's personal information, and maps to addresses associated with his family, according to court documents.

Lucy Richards, an avowed Infowars listener, subsequently went to prison for issuing repeated death threats against Mr. Pozner. The Pozner family lives in hiding, and is suing Mr. Jones for defamation.

On Father's Day 2017, Mr. Jones went on Infowars in a brief broadcast to offer the Sandy Hook parents "my sincere condolences" for the loss of their children in "the horrible tragedy" in Newtown, Conn. He said he wanted to "open a dialogue" with the families because it was essential for the nation to come together rather than "letting the MSM misrepresent things," referring to the mainstream media.

In the Times interview, Mr. Jones suggested that blame for the pain of the Sandy Hook families rests not with him but with the media and inconsistencies in coverage of the shooting.

"I was covering a giant phenomenon of people not believing media anymore because they've been caught in governments' lying so much," he said.

Alex Jones grew up in a conservative, upper-middle-class family in the Dallas suburb of Rockwall, the son of a dentist.

There was nothing particularly unusual about him during those days, except a conspiratorial nature and, from high school on, as he put it in court testimony, a commitment to "seeking out ways to get on air."

Mr. Jones was inspired, he has said, by "None Dare Call It Conspiracy," a 1971 book by Gary Allen that advanced the conservative theory that domestic decision making is not guided by elected officials, but international bankers and politicians. Mr. Allen also sold similarly-themed recordings by mail order.

While a community college student in Austin, Mr. Jones landed a show on Austin community access cable hawking outlandish conspiracy theories.

When Kelly Jones met him in Austin in the late 1990s, Mr. Jones was wearing a bumblebee costume in the Texas heat, doing promotional stunts for a local radio station.

He dropped out of community college, and with money from his father, produced "documentary" videos, starring himself, about 9/11 being an inside job, "police state" abuses and the "new world order" he claimed was being engineered by the Bilderberg Group, an annual gathering of prominent financiers, economists and political leaders.

He bought airtime on shortwave radio, and broadcast his theories out of an unused nursery in his house with "choo-choo" train wallpaper, Ms. Jones said in an interview.

To the extent that his early shows were informed by coherent political thought, he was a libertarian, suspicious of Republicans and Democrats alike; Ron Paul, the three-time presidential candidate and libertarian icon, was an occasional guest.

But with the election of President Barack Obama in 2008, Mr. Jones discovered that nasty partisanship was a moneymaker.

In court in 2014, he said, "We have had company meetings in the last two years preparing for the eventuality of a Republican takeover," which he considered a threat to his business, because when attacking Democrats in power, conservatives could "be more provocative, more interesting and so it gets more viewers."

Mr. Trump, who entered electoral politics spreading the false assertion that Mr. Obama might not have been born in the United States, was a welcome surprise for Mr. Jones. He found in Mr. Trump a kindred anti-intellectual with an outsider's perspective and a willingness to entertain conspiracy theories and disseminate fact-challenged assertions.

The two men were connected by Roger Stone, a longtime adviser to Mr. Trump who is a paid host on Infowars. In December 2015 Mr. Stone arranged for Mr. Trump to do a 30-minute interview with Mr. Jones.

The themes promoted by Mr. Jones sometimes make their way through the media ecosystem and win the attention of Mr. Trump, like a bogus assertion about the slaughter of white farmers in South Africa that the president invoked last month. In the wake of steps by the social media companies to ban Mr. Jones, the president has also repeatedly voiced concerns nearly identical to those expressed by Mr. Jones about efforts by technology companies to silence voices from the right.

On Infowars last month, Mr. Jones suggested that he is coordinating his message with Mr. Trump.

"We advise the president," Mr. Jones said. "We've got all the documents. We've got the proof. Other people are scared to tell him what's going on."

Two White House officials said they were not aware of any recent contacts between Mr. Jones and the president.

Infowars operates through a series of interlocking companies, none of which publicly reports its results. But a rough picture of the operation's scale can be gleaned from the documents detailing its financial condition in 2014.

One entity — created to house the supplements business — generated sales of $15.6 million and net income of $5 million from October 2013 through September 2014, according to an unaudited profit and loss statement viewed by The Times. During the same period, another entity, possibly recording overlapping revenues, listed net income of $2.9 million and sales of $14.3 million, with merchandise sales accounting for $10 million, advertising for nearly $2 million and $53,350.66 in donations, according to an unaudited company statement.

Since then, current and former business associates said, the Infowars empire has continued to thrive.

The heart of the business is sales of lightly regulated nutritional supplements that purport to improve health or virility or both.

"Supplements are popular," Mr. Jones said in the interview. "They're good. They're a fast-growing market. I use it to fund the operation. Other revolutionaries rob banks and kidnap people, O.K.? I don't do that."

By late 2012, Mr. Jones decided to create a supplement line of his own, a move that would allow him to reap more of the profits. The next

ALYSSA SCHUKAR FOR THE NEW YORK TIMES

A supplement called “Advanced Liver Cleanse Pack” sold by Infowars.

summer, he recruited his father, David R. Jones, to leave his dental practice and help manage the family business, negotiating a deal for Dr. Jones to be paid what he was making previously — $300,000 to $500,000 a year — plus an additional bonus of 20 percent of the profits from the entities he created.

When Dr. Jones came on board, the business was in disarray. In court testimony, he said he found a series of “green notebooks stuck in a cabinet” outlining a number of entities that had been established over the years.

Dr. Jones set about evaluating the business, getting the corporate entities sorted out, and creating opportunities to expand the supplement business.

The company struck deals with a number of manufacturers, slapping its Infowars Life label on a range of products. A 2014 agreement with one of its most prominent suppliers, Global Healing Center, shows that the manufacturer made at least eight products for the brand, including “Super Male Vitality” a private label of Global Health’s Androtrex, purchased wholesale for $14.99 and advertised on the Infowars Store for $69.95.

Kelly Jones compared Mr. Jones’s marketing to that of a televangelist, preaching to his faithful, selling cures and soliciting donations. His customers buy in — and then they buy. For every threat he raises, there is a solution for sale.

Matt Redhawk is the founder of My Patriot Supply. The company sells water filtration systems, emergency survival food and other products on Infowars targeting consumers in the preparedness movement, “from someone who is preparing for a job loss or a weekend without power, up to the full blown Armageddon,” Mr. Redhawk said in an interview.

“Controversy sells. You can’t ignore the fact that there is a method there,” he said.

“Preppers” are an important market segment for Infowars, and ads on its website bring better response than on other conservative media shows, said Chad Cooper, who owns Infidel Body Armor, based in San Tan Valley, Ariz. He spent about $5,000 a month on Infowars advertising for his civilian body armor line until recently, when he suspended his advertising because Infowars started selling ads to too many of his competitors.

While he does not take in Mr. Jones’s show — “he’s a nutter,” he says — “I’ve spent quite a bit of time on the phone with these Alex Jones people who order from me,” and described them.

“They’re nonbelievers in what the media tells them. They think there’s more to the story,” he said. “They think there’s aliens, and the government knows about that and they’re not telling them. They’re all religious, and they’re very concerned about the direction the government is going.”

“He’s really good at scaring people,” Mr. Cooper said of Mr. Jones. “He gives them that sense of urgency — they need to hurry up and do something. Now.”

Last February, two former employees came forward with allegations that they faced discrimination at Infowars. In interviews, they depicted Mr. Jones as the leader of a racially charged workplace.

Robert A. Jacobson, 43, started working with Mr. Jones in 2004 as a video editor, and said that over the years he was taunted for being Jewish. He said that the harassment escalated after August 2015 when Mr. Jones interviewed David Duke, the former Ku Klux Klan grand wizard.

Ashley L. Beckford, who was hired as a production assistant in June 2016, said that she was called racial slurs, paid less because of the color of her skin and forced to fend off unwanted sexual advances, including from Mr. Jones. Ms. Beckford, 32, said that an employee once called her a "coon," that she was shown swastikas in the office, that Mr. Jones once grabbed her buttocks, and that staff members repeatedly used the term "fat black bitch" around her.

On his show, Mr. Jones denied the allegations and called both former employees liars.

Mr. Jones's image and credibility as a provocateur are closely linked to his credibility as a marketer of supplements and other products.

Consequently, sales of the fluoride-free toothpaste he promotes might decline if he recants his bogus claim that fluoridated water causes cancer and stunts the brains of children. Demand for Infowars-branded gun components that can be purchased without a firearms permit might fall if he backs off his predictions of a looming civil war.

Mr. Jones had cited a desire to express contrition to the Sandy Hook parents as a reason for agreeing to be interviewed. But many times during the interview, his efforts at apology morphed into new theories.

"The idea they're pushing is that you can't ever question anything," he said, "they" referring to anyone who criticizes his twisting of the truth. "I don't think you can establish that anything is 100 percent fact."

JACK NICAS and **KITTY BENNETT** contributed reporting.

‘Crisis Actor’ Isn’t a New Smear. The Idea of Paid Protesters Goes Back to the Civil War Era.

BY NIRAJ CHOKSHI | FEB. 24, 2018

AFTER ANY MAJOR ATTACK, you are likely to find in some dark corner of the internet conspiracy theories that the survivors or victims made it all up or were part of a troupe of paid “crisis actors.”

Such theories emerged after the massacres in Las Vegas in October; at a gay nightclub in Orlando, Fla., in 2016; and at Sandy Hook Elementary School in Newtown, Conn., in 2012. It happened again in February, after 17 people were killed in the school shooting in Parkland, Fla.

Those conspiracy theories have been amplified in the internet age, but they are a part of a long, troubled history of dismissing the voices of those seeking change.

“This theme that anyone agitating for change must be either an outside agitator or must have been paid or put up to it is one that runs throughout American history,” Kevin M. Kruse, a history professor at Princeton University, said in a phone interview.

Conspiracies of this kind quickly circulated about the Florida shooting, with one top-trending YouTube video suggesting, falsely, that one of the survivors was a hired actor. The video’s caption tapped into the idea that student protesters were paid to advocate gun control, and Mr. Kruse pointed his followers on Twitter to a decades-old analog: In 1957, civil rights supporters had to dispel rumors that nine black children seeking to integrate Central High School in Little Rock, Ark., were being paid for their activism.

That strategy of dismissing protest as being funded or imported by outsiders was commonly used during the civil rights movement to minimize racial tension or brush aside genuine demands for equality.

"It's a perennial theme of segregationists that this activism is not sincere, that it's not Americans advocating for their own rights but rather it's a scam," Mr. Kruse said.

In his 1963 "Letter From a Birmingham Jail" defending nonviolent civil disobedience, the Rev. Dr. Martin Luther King Jr. described the tactic as an effort to silence African-American voices.

"If our white brothers dismiss as 'rabble rousers' and 'outside agitators' those of us who employ nonviolent direct action, and if they refuse to support our nonviolent efforts, millions of Negroes will, out of frustration and despair, seek solace and security in black nationalist ideologies — a development that would inevitably lead to a frightening racial nightmare," Dr. King wrote.

Politicians of that era often promoted the idea of the "outside agitator" to portray racial discord as isolated and exaggerated, but they hardly invented the strategy.

Similar tactics were used in the years after the Civil War to minimize stories of the violence and discrimination faced by African-Americans, Heather Cox Richardson, a history professor at Boston College, said in a phone interview.

As the nation began the process of postwar reunification, some in Congress invited testimony from African-Americans, offering them a per diem to cover travel costs and missed wages, she said. But those seeking to dismiss their stories of pain and demands for equality argued that the payments were proof that their accounts could not be trusted.

"You get this idea immediately after the war, during these testimonies, that people talking about civil rights are literally getting paid" to tell fabricated stories, Ms. Richardson said.

That belief spread to other contexts, too. Testimony from African-Americans on the violence perpetrated by the Ku Klux Klan, for example, was explained away as funded falsehoods.

"They were attracted by a fee of two dollars per diem, and in many cases were evidently drilled for the occasion," one politician said of the testimony, according to an 1871 news report. The accounts, he said, were "of the lowest kind and utterly unworthy of belief."

To Ms. Richardson, those early dismissals of African-American testimony, starting with the congressional hearings during the Reconstruction era, are not unlike the false theories spread about the Parkland school shooting suggesting that the student survivors were actors paid to protest for gun control.

"That actually sounds very much like what you got in those first congressional hearings," she said.

Glossary

Antifa A left-wing political protest movement made up of groups unified by their opposition to fascism and extreme right-wing ideology.

birther An individual who subscribes to the incorrect belief that President Barack Obama was born outside the United States and therefore ineligible to be president.

cabal A secret group or political faction.

cognitive dissonance The state of having thoughts and beliefs that are inconsistent or contradictory.

controlled demolition The act of wrecking or destroying particularly by explosives. Believed in 9/11 conspiracy circles to be the cause for the collapse of the World Trade Center.

crisis actor A trained actor used to portray a disaster victim during emergency drills for rescue workers. Used in conspiracy circles to refer to individuals who are paid by the government to deceive the public with tales of trauma and suffering.

deep state A term that refers to a clandestine group in government that holds political influence.

disseminate To spread information widely.

false flag Relates to naval warfare when a ship would fly a flag that would conceal its true identity as a way to lure an enemy closer. Today, it is commonly a shorthand for an act of deception and is used by conspiracy theorists to label high-profile attacks.

hoax A humorous or malicious deception; a story intended to deceive or to defraud.

hyperbole An extreme exaggeration; a rhetorical device that overstates and is not meant to be taken literally.

insinuation An indirect hint or a suggestion that something is bad or wrong.

misinformation False or inaccurate information designed to mislead and deceive an audience.

paranoia The irrational belief that one is being persecuted or conspired against.

pathological Behavior caused by illness or disease; behavior that is compulsive or obsessive in nature.

patsy A person who is easily taken advantage of, especially someone who can be blamed for something.

polemic An aggressive attack on someone else's beliefs or ideas; promotion of controversy.

QAnon A far-right conspiracy theory that suggests a deep state plot against President Donald Trump.

scrutinize To examine or inspect thoroughly or closely.

truther A person who doubts the publicly accepted view of an event, believing that a conspiracy exists to conceal the true explanation. Usually used to refer to 9/11 conspiracy theorists.

WikiLeaks An international nonprofit run by Julian Assange that publishes secret information, news leaks and classified information.

Media Literacy Terms

"Media literacy" refers to the ability to access, understand, critically assess and create media. The following terms are important components of media literacy, and they will help you critically engage with the articles in this title.

angle The aspect of a news story that a journalist focuses on and develops.

attribution The method by which a source is identified or by which facts and information are assigned to the person who provided them.

balance Principle of journalism that both perspectives of an argument should be presented in a fair way.

bias A disposition of prejudice in favor of a certain idea, person or perspective.

credibility The quality of being trustworthy and believable, said of a journalistic source.

editorial Article of opinion or interpretation.

fake news A fictional or made-up story presented in the style of a legitimate news story, intended to deceive readers; also commonly used to criticize legitimate news because of its perspective or unfavorable coverage of a subject.

feature story Article designed to entertain as well as to inform.

headline Type, usually 18 point or larger, used to introduce a story.

impartiality Principle of journalism that a story should not reflect a journalist's bias and should contain balance.

intention The motive or reason behind something, such as the publication of a news story.

interview story A type of story in which the facts are gathered primarily by interviewing another person or persons.

inverted pyramid A method of writing a story using facts in order of importance, beginning with a lead and then gradually adding paragraphs in order of relevance from most interesting to least interesting.

motive The reason behind something, such as the publication of a news story or a source's perspective on an issue.

news story An article or style of expository writing that reports news, generally in a straightforward fashion and without editorial comment.

op-ed An opinion piece that reflects a prominent individual's opinion on a topic of interest.

paraphrase The summary of an individual's words, with attribution, rather than a direct quotation of their exact words.

quotation The use of an individual's exact words indicated by the use of quotation marks and proper attribution.

reliability The quality of being dependable and accurate, said of a journalistic source.

rhetorical device Technique in writing intending to persuade the reader or communicate a message from a certain perspective.

source The origin of the information reported in journalism.

tone A manner of expression in writing or speech.

Media Literacy Questions

1. Identify the various sources cited in the article "Conspiracy Theories Made Alex Jones Very Rich. They May Bring Him Down." (on page 196). How do the journalists attribute information to each of these sources in the article? How effective are their attributions in helping the reader identify their sources?

2. In "After Orlando Shooting, 'False Flag' and 'Crisis Actor' Conspiracy Theories Surface" (on page 159), Christopher Mele paraphrases information from Jesse Walker. What are the strengths of the use of a paraphrase as opposed to a direct quote? What are the weaknesses?

3. Compare the headlines of "The Demented Detectives on Seth Rich's Case" (on page 79) and "Even as He Rises, Donald Trump Entertains Conspiracy Theories" (on page 111). Which is a more compelling headline, and why? How could the less compelling headline be changed to better draw the reader's interest?

4. Do Ashley Parker and Steve Eder demonstrate the journalistic principle of impartiality in their article "Inside the Six Weeks Donald Trump Was a Nonstop 'Birther' " (on page 116)? If so, how did they do so? If not, what could they have included to make their article more impartial?

5. The article "Did You Hear the Latest About Hillary?" (on page 69) is an example of an op-ed. Identify how Zeynep Tufekci's attitude and tone help convey her opinion on the topic.

6. Does "He Calls Hillary Clinton a 'Demon.' Who Is Alex Jones?" (on page 163) use multiple sources? What are the strengths of using multiple sources in a journalistic piece? What are the weaknesses of relying heavily on only one or a few sources?

7. What is the intention of the article "How the Murder of a D.N.C. Staff Member Fueled Conspiracy Theories" (on page 75)? How effectively does it achieve its intended purpose?

8. Analyze the authors' reporting in "500 Conspiracy Buffs Meet to Seek the Truth of 9/11" (on page 46) and "As Donald Trump Pushes Conspiracy Theories, Right-Wing Media Gets Its Wish" (on page 127). Do you think one journalist is more balanced in their reporting than the other? If so, why do you think so?

9. Often, as a news story develops, a journalist's attitude toward the subject may change. Compare "Sean Hannity, a Murder and Why Fake News Endures" (on page 83) and "You Don't Need to Go to the Dark Web to Find Hateful Conspiracy Theories" (on page 101), both by Jim Rutenberg. Did new information discovered between the publication of these two articles change Rutenberg's perspective?

10. Identify each of the sources in "What Is QAnon: Explaining the Internet Conspiracy Theory That Showed Up at a Trump Rally" (on page 91) as a primary source or a secondary source. Evaluate the reliability and credibility of each source. How does your evaluation of each source change your perspective on this article?

Citations

All citations in this list are formatted according to the Modern Language Association's (MLA) style guide.

BOOK CITATION

THE NEW YORK TIMES EDITORIAL STAFF. *Conspiracy Theories: Real, Imagined and Manufactured.* New York Times Educational Publishing, 2020.

ONLINE ARTICLE CITATIONS

BAKER, PETER, AND MAGGIE HABERMAN. "A Conspiracy Theory's Journey From Talk Radio to Trump's Twitter." *The New York Times*, 5 Mar. 2017, www.nytimes.com/2017/03/05/us/politics/trump-twitter-talk-radio-conspiracy-theory.html.

BAKER, PETER, AND SCOTT SHANE. "J.F.K. Files, Though Incomplete, Are a Treasure Trove for Answer Seekers." *The New York Times*, 26 Oct. 2017, www.nytimes.com/2017/10/26/us/politics/trump-jfk-release.html.

BANK, JUSTIN, ET AL. "What Is QAnon: Explaining the Internet Conspiracy Theory That Showed Up at a Trump Rally." *The New York Times*, 1 Aug. 2018, www.nytimes.com/2018/08/01/us/politics/what-is-qanon.html.

BARBARO, MICHAEL. "Donald Trump Clung to 'Birther' Lie for Years, and Still Isn't Apologetic." *The New York Times*, 16 Sept. 2016, www.nytimes.com/2016/09/17/us/politics/donald-trump-obama-birther.html.

BARRY, DAN. "Mystery From the Grave Beside Oswald's, Solved." *The New York Times*, 9 Aug. 2013, www.nytimes.com/2013/08/10/us/mystery-from-the-grave-beside-oswalds-solved.html.

BARRY, DAN. "No Stranger to Conspiracy." *The New York Times*, 17 Aug. 2013, www.nytimes.com/2013/08/18/opinion/sunday/no-stranger-to-conspiracy.html.

BROMWICH, JONAH ENGEL. "How the Murder of a D.N.C. Staff Member Fueled Conspiracy Theories." *The New York Times*, 17 May 2017, www.nytimes.com/2017/05/17/us/seth-rich-dnc-wikileaks.html.

BROMWICH, JONAH ENGEL. "YouTube Cracks Down on Far-Right Videos as Conspiracy Theories Spread." *The New York Times*, 3 Mar. 2018, www.nytimes.com/2018/03/03/technology/youtube-right-wing-channels.html.

CHOKSHI, NIRAJ. " 'Crisis Actor' Isn't a New Smear. The Idea of Paid Protesters Goes Back to the Civil War Era." *The New York Times*, 24 Feb. 2018, www.nytimes.com/2018/02/24/us/crisis-actors-florida-shooting.html.

DAVIS, JULIE HIRSCHFELD, AND MAGGIE HABERMAN. "With 'Spygate,' Trump Shows How He Uses Conspiracy Theories to Erode Trust." *The New York Times*, 28 May 2018, www.nytimes.com/2018/05/28/us/politics/trump-conspiracy-theories-spygate.html.

DWYER, JIM. "Drawing a Line From Alternative Theories to Untruths." *The New York Times*, 7 Feb. 2017, www.nytimes.com/2017/02/07/nyregion/donald-trump-infowars.html.

DWYER, JIM. "2 U.S. Reports Seek to Counter Conspiracy Theories About 9/11." *The New York Times*, 2 Jan. 2006, www.nytimes.com/2006/09/02/nyregion/02conspiracy.html.

FEUER, ALAN. "500 Conspiracy Buffs Meet to Seek the Truth of 9/11." *The New York Times*, 5 June 2006, www.nytimes.com/2006/06/05/us/05conspiracy.html.

FRENKEL, SHEERA, AND DAISUKE WAKABAYASHI. "After Florida School Shooting, Russian 'Bot' Army Pounced." *The New York Times*, 19 Feb. 2018, www.nytimes.com/2018/02/19/technology/russian-bots-school-shooting.html.

GOLDBERG, MICHELLE. "The Conspiracy Theory That Says Trump Is a Genius." *The New York Times*, 6 Apr. 2018, www.nytimes.com/2018/04/06/opinion/qanon-trump-conspiracy-theory.html.

GRYNBAUM, MICHAEL M. "Las Vegas Massacre Gives InfoWars More Conspiracy Fodder." *The New York Times*, 9 Oct. 2017, www.nytimes.com/2017/10/09/business/media/las-vegas-massacre-infowars-conspiracy.html.

GRYNBAUM, MICHAEL M. "Right-Wing Media Uses Parkland Shooting as Conspiracy Fodder." *The New York Times*, 20 Feb. 2018, www.nytimes.com/2018/02/20/business/media/parkland-shooting-media-conspiracy.html.

HABERMAN, CLYDE. "Who's Fueling Conspiracy Whisperers' Falsehoods?" *The New York Times*, 30 Apr. 2017, www.nytimes.com/2017/04/30/us/retro-report-conspiracy-theories-kennedy-trump.html.

HABERMAN, MAGGIE. "Even as He Rises, Donald Trump Entertains Conspiracy Theories." *The New York Times*, 29 Feb. 2016, www.nytimes.com/2016

/03/01/us/politics/donald-trump-conspiracy-theories.html.

HEILBRUNN, JACOB. "Inside the World of Conspiracy Theorists." *The New York Times*, 13 May 2011, www.nytimes.com/2011/05/15/books/review/book-review-among-the-truthers-by-jonathan-kay.html.

HERRMAN, JOHN. "The Making of a No. 1 YouTube Conspiracy Video After the Parkland Tragedy." *The New York Times*, 21 Feb. 2018, www.nytimes.com/2018/02/21/business/media/youtube-conspiracy-video-parkland.html.

KEARSE, STEPHEN. "Wild Speculation Isn't Worth Much. A 'Theory,' However …" *The New York Times*, 19 Dec. 2018, www.nytimes.com/2018/12/19/magazine/wild-speculation-isnt-worth-much-a-theory-however.html.

KILGANNON, COREY. "9/11 'Truthers' to Tone Protests Down, for a Day." *The New York Times*, 9 Sept. 2011, cityroom.blogs.nytimes.com/2011/09/09/911-truthers-to-tone-protests-down-for-a-day/.

KRAUSS, CLIFFORD. "28 Years After Kennedy's Assassination, Conspiracy Theories Refuse to Die." *The New York Times*, 5 Jan. 1992, www.nytimes.com/1992/01/05/us/28-years-after-kennedy-s-assassination-conspiracy-theories-refuse-to-die.html.

LEIBOVICH, MARK. "The Weaponization of 'Truther.' " *The New York Times*, 4 Nov. 2015, www.nytimes.com/2015/11/08/magazine/the-weaponization-of-truther.html.

LIPTON, ERIC. "Man Motivated by 'Pizzagate' Conspiracy Theory Arrested in Washington Gunfire." *The New York Times*, 5 Dec. 2016, www.nytimes.com/2016/12/05/us/pizzagate-comet-ping-pong-edgar-maddison-welch.html.

MARTIN, JONATHAN. "As Donald Trump Pushes Conspiracy Theories, Right-Wing Media Gets Its Wish." *The New York Times*, 25 May 2016, www.nytimes.com/2016/05/26/us/politics/donald-trump-presidential-race.html.

MELE, CHRISTOPHER. "After Orlando Shooting, 'False Flag' and 'Crisis Actor' Conspiracy Theories Surface." *The New York Times*, 28 June 2016, www.nytimes.com/2016/06/29/us/after-orlando-shooting-false-flag-and-crisis-actor-conspiracy-theories-surface.html.

MERLAN, ANNA. "The Demented Detectives on Seth Rich's Case." *The New York Times*, 26 May 2017, www.nytimes.com/2017/05/26/opinion/seth-rich-conspiracy-theory-fox-news.html.

MOORE, LORI. "The J.F.K. Files: Decades of Doubts and Conspiracy Theories." *The New York Times*, 25 Oct. 2017, www.nytimes.com/2017/10/25/us/jfk-assassination-files-questions.html.

NICAS, JACK, AND SHEERA FRENKEL. "Facebook and Google Struggle to Squelch 'Crisis Actor' Posts." *The New York Times*, 23 Feb. 2018, www.nytimes.com/2018/02/23/technology/trolls-step-ahead-facebook-youtube-florida-shooting.html.

PARKER, ASHLEY, AND STEVE EDER. "Inside the Six Weeks Donald Trump Was a Nonstop 'Birther.' " *The New York Times*, 2 July 2016, www.nytimes.com/2016/07/03/us/politics/donald-trump-birther-obama.html.

PETERS, JEREMY W. "How Trump-Fed Conspiracy Theories About Migrant Caravan Intersect With Deadly Hatred." *The New York Times*, 29 Oct. 2018, www.nytimes.com/2018/10/29/us/politics/caravan-trump-shooting-elections.html.

QIU, LINDA. "Did Democrats, or George Soros, Fund Migrant Caravan? Despite Republican Claims, No." *The New York Times*, 20 Oct. 2018, www.nytimes.com/2018/10/20/world/americas/migrant-caravan-video-trump.html.

ROBERTSON, CAMPBELL. "In Donald Trump, Conspiracy Fans Find a Campaign to Believe In." *The New York Times*, 17 Oct. 2017, www.nytimes.com/2016/10/18/us/in-donald-trump-conspiracy-fans-find-a-campaign-to-believe-in.html.

RUTENBERG, JIM. "Sean Hannity, a Murder and Why Fake News Endures." *The New York Times*, 24 May 2017, www.nytimes.com/2017/05/24/business/media/seth-rich-fox-news-sean-hannity.html.

RUTENBERG, JIM. "You Don't Need to Go to the Dark Web to Find Hateful Conspiracy Theories." *The New York Times*, 31 Oct. 2018, www.nytimes.com/2018/10/31/business/media/dark-web-conspiracy-theories.html.

SCHWARTZ, MATTATHIAS. "A Trail of 'Bread Crumbs,' Leading Conspiracy Theorists Into the Wilderness." *The New York Times*, 11 Sept. 2018, www.nytimes.com/2018/09/11/magazine/a-trail-of-bread-crumbs-leading-conspiracy-theorists-into-the-wilderness.html.

SHEAR, MICHAEL D., AND EILEEN SULLIVAN. "Trump Attacks Sessions and F.B.I., Citing Conspiracy Theories." *The New York Times*, 19 Sept. 2018, www.nytimes.com/2018/09/19/us/politics/jeff-sessions-attorney-general-trump.html.

STACK, LIAM. "He Calls Hillary Clinton a 'Demon.' Who Is Alex Jones?" *The New York Times*, 13 Oct. 2016, www.nytimes.com/2016/10/14/us/politics/alex-jones.html.

TUFEKCI, ZEYNEP. "Did You Hear the Latest About Hillary?" *The New York Times*, 12 Sept. 2016, www.nytimes.com/2016/09/13/opinion

/campaign-stops/did-you-hear-the-latest-about-hillary.html.

VICTOR, DANIEL. "A J.F.K. Assassination Glossary: Key Figures and Theories." *The New York Times*, 26 Oct. 2017, www.nytimes.com/2017/10/26/us/jfk-assassination.html.

WILLIAMSON, ELIZABETH. "Alex Jones, Pursued Over Infowars Falsehoods, Faces a Legal Crossroads." *The New York Times*, 31 July 2018, www.nytimes.com/2018/07/31/us/politics/alex-jones-defamation-suit-sandy-hook.html.

WILLIAMSON, ELIZABETH, AND EMILY STEEL. "Conspiracy Theories Made Alex Jones Very Rich. They May Bring Him Down." *The New York Times*, 7 Sept. 2018, www.nytimes.com/2018/09/07/us/politics/alex-jones-business-infowars-conspiracy.html.

Index

This book is current up until the time of printing. For the most up-to-date reporting, visit www.nytimes.com.